D1135276

111447854

PAPER CRAFT school

PAPER CRAFT school

CLIVE STEVENS

Reader's Digest

PUBLISHED BY THE READER'S DIGEST ASSOCIATION LIMITED
LONDON • NEW YORK • SYDNEY • CAPE TOWN • MONTREAL

Published by The Reader's Digest Association Limited
Berkeley Square House
Berkeley Square
London W1X 6AB

ISBN 0–276–42242–2

This book was designed and produced by
Quarto Publishing plc
The Old Brewery
6 Blundell Street
London N7 9BH

Senior Art Editor *Penny Cobb*
Senior Editors *Sian Parkhouse, Sally MacEachern*
Text Editor *Mary Senechal*
Designer *Sheila Volpe*
Picture Researcher *Susannah Jayes*
Picture Manager *Giulia Hetherington*
Photographers *Laura Wickenden, Paul Forrester*
Illustrations *Dave Kemp*
Editorial Director *Mark Dartford*
Art Director *Moira Clinch*

Typeset in Great Britain by Central Southern Typesetters
Manufactured in Singapore by Eray Scan Pte Ltd
Printed in Singapore by Star Standard Industries (Pte) Ltd

Foreword

At some time in their lives everyone has used
paper as an art medium: to draw and paint
on, to make a collage, to construct three-
dimensional forms from cut-out shapes or papier
mâché. In fact, paper is probably the most versatile
art material there is. There are so many different
art forms based on paper that we could not include
them all in this book. Rather, we concentrate on
those that use the paper itself as the medium,
from simple weaving and collage to more ambi-
tious art forms, such as advanced pop-ups and

paper sculpture. All of the basic techniques are straightforward and easy to accomplish. By trying the projects in order you will be guided through a series of achievements that increase in complexity as you proceed, leaving you with all the skills necessary to create your own original paper masterpieces.

Working with paper can be very absorbing, and it is an ideal medium for all ages. Paper is readily available and inexpensive, and paper crafts need little special equipment.

As you proceed through the book, pay special attention to the details in the exciting works of the artists featured on the gallery pages and discover their wonderful techniques. By trying these you will find your own individual style.

Clive Stevens

Contents

Introduction

Paper is a material that most of us take for granted today. We use it to record the world's knowledge, print the morning news, write financial transactions, wrap food and decorate our homes, to name but a few of its many applications. Attributed to the Chinese, paper was invented during the Han dynasty (202 B.C. to A.D. 220). But the art of papermaking remained a closely guarded secret for almost 500 years, and its spread throughout the rest of the world was very slow. It was not until the seventh century that it was introduced into Japan through Korea, at about the same time as Buddhism.

Originally, paper had an important role in religion, utilized for its symbolic purity and for the distribution of holy texts. Gradually, it began to be used for practical purposes, such as floor coverings and sail cloths, sliding screens, masks, kites and even clothing.

It was the Arabs who took paper to the rest of the world. Having captured the secret of paper-making along with the Chinese prisoners they took during an attack on the city of Samarkand in A.D. 751, they developed their own manufacturing sites, and began exporting paper to Europe. The paper industry started in Spain but by the fifteenth century, production was widespread throughout Europe, and paper had completely replaced papyrus, parchment, and vellum as a writing material.

ORIGAMI AND PAPERCUTS

From very early in its history paper was exploited for its aesthetic as well as for its functional qualities. Used by artists as a surface on which to produce art, it was also a medium in its own right. One of the most familiar and instantly recognizable forms of paper arts is origami. It is a matter of dispute whether origami originated in Japan, Korea, or China, but we do know that the Japanese were producing sophisticated forms

NEWSPRINT
Newspapers are generally made from cheap, poor-quality pulp with a high acid content. Newsprint differs in colour and tends to turn brown over time.

HANDMADE PAPER PRODUCTION
This photograph of Whatman's famous Springfield Paper Mill, taken circa 1905, shows the former dipping the mould and deckle in the vat and the coucher waiting behind the blankets, ready to couch the freshly formed sheet.

some 1200 years ago. The word itself is Japanese, from *ori* (to fold) and *kami* (paper). The popularity of the art died out until the 1930s, when a young Japanese man called Akira Yoshizawa began developing new forms based on old designs. Unlike the traditional form of origami, which allowed the paper to be cut as well as folded, the newer forms kept to strict rules that demanded that all shapes should be created from a single piece of paper using folds only. The popularity of origami spread to the West and was confirmed by the publication in 1956 of a British book called *Paper Magic* by the South African Robert Harbin and later books by an American, Samuel Randlett.

Some of the earliest forms of paper art are Chinese paper cuts dating from the twelfth century AD. These were used to adorn paper-covered windows. Polish paper cuts date from around the same time. Traditionally made by peasant women, they were used to decorate the home. Different techniques were specific to different regions, so that the source of a design could be identified by whether it was created using two folds, which produced four identical squares, or one fold, which created bilateral symmetry. Paper cutting also had a tradition in many other

ORIGINS OF ORIGAMI
Origami in Japan dates back 1200 years. This eighteenth century painting shows the courtesan Segawa of the Ogiya (house) holding a paper crane – a classic origami design. (Utamaro, from the series 'Yukun Waka Sannin').

MODERN PAPER-CUT
This amazingly intricate paper-cut is based on a well-known Chinese literary classic. The artist used Chinese calligraphy paper, a craft knife and a pointed pair of Chinese scissors (collection of David Chu).

parts of the world, particularly the Netherlands, and areas of the United States with a strong Dutch influence, such as Pennsylvania. The subject matter often included pastoral scenes and family groups.

PAPER SCULPTURE AND POP-UPS

It is believed that modern paper sculpture originated in Poland. After seeing the works of Polish artists in continental exhibitions, English and American artists became influenced by it. Many Polish artists emigrated to America taking their talents with them. In the 1940s and 1950s big department stores seized on paper sculpture as a versatile and exciting new means of creating window displays that were relatively quick to construct, had an architectural effect and were inexpensive. Advertising agencies too were quick to recognize the appeal and effectiveness of paper sculpture and it was used in numerous campaigns. Although its popularity died down, there was renewed interest in the 1970s. Today it is an enormously popular art form.

Another paper art form that has been exploited by the advertising and graphic arts industry is pop-ups. A specialised form of paper sculpture, pop-ups were first used in children's books during the latter half of the nineteenth century. They were very expensive to produce however, and so they declined in popularity until the 1950s, when much innovative work was done

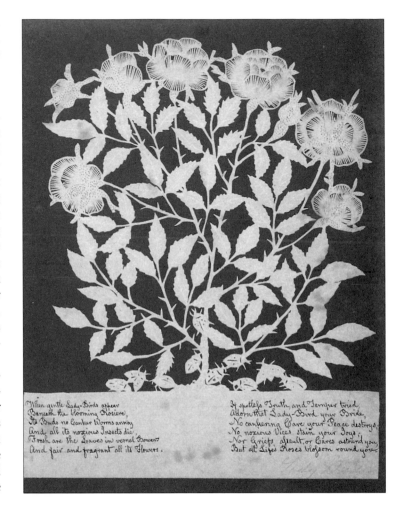

When gentle Lady-Birds appear
Beneath the blooming Rosiere,
Its Buds no Canker Worms annoy
And all its noxious Insects die
Fresh are the Leaves in vernal Bowers
And fair and fragrant all its Flowers.

If spotless Truth and Temper tried,
Adorn that Lady-Bird your Bride,
No cankering Care your Peace destroys,
No noxious Vices stain your Joys,
Nor Griefs assault or Cares astound you
But all Life's Roses blossom round you

HISTORICAL PAPER-CUT

This fine paper-cut was executed with a sharp knife. Note how the artist achieved intricate petal detail using a series of delicate cutouts (collection of Nancy Rosin).

DÉCOUPAGE

This attractive perfume box is a typical example of nineteenth century découpage. The many layers of varnish give it a lacquered finish.

in Czechoslovakia. American and British publishers were inspired to create their own books, and with the development of more sophisticated printing techniques, costs were lowered sufficiently for pop-ups to be produced on a large scale. It was not long before greetings card manufacturers began to use pop-ups, and the medium was explored and developed to create the huge variety of complex and ingenious designs available.

Today, paper artists have even more to inspire them. They can draw on traditional and historical techniques, like those described in this book, and either practise them in their purest forms, or adapt them bringing modern design values and style to their work. And never before has there been a greater range of paper types, weights, colours and textures available, as you can see in the 'Directory of Papers' on pages 16 to 21. Paper is an inspiration in itself, to be admired for its own innate beauty, and also as a medium for creating stunning works of art.

POP-UP ADVERTISEMENT
This fine example of a magic box mechanism dates from circa 1910. As the card is opened the teacups and loaf of bread rise up from the table (Robert Opie).

POP-UP BOOK
These pop-up books from the 1930s make use of two mechanisms: a multiple layer mechanism on the left and a V-fold on the right (Robert Opie).

1
Materials

Paper

MATERIALS

Paper is available in a wide variety of types. The 'Directory of Papers' on pages 16–21 contains specific advice on which type is best suited for the particular application you have in mind. But paper is a ubiquitous medium. We encounter it in numerous different forms every day, and it is helpful to have some knowledge about its general nature.

The papers we most commonly come into contact with are newsprint and bond. Newsprint, a low-grade paper made from mechanical pulp, or groundwood, is used for printing newspapers. Groundwood is made by grinding peeled logs in a stream of water until the wood is broken down into fibres. It is an ideal medium for papermaking and papier mâché.

Bond is made in a wide variety of qualities, the highest quality from 100 per cent rag pulp, and the lower-grade stocks from greater proportions of groundwood. Bond paper is sized (sealed with a glue mixture) to prevent penetration by writing and drawing inks and is commonly used as stationery in offices. It is a versatile paper and can be used when the project you are working on does not require specific qualities.

Other common terms that you will come across when buying paper are *coated*, *rag*, *laid* and *wove*. Coated papers have been specially treated with a surface coating to improve their printing quality. Rag papers are made from a high percentage of fibre from cotton or linen rags and so are of a very high quality. Rag papers are often used for watercolour painting. Laid and wove refer to the appearance of the paper, which results from the way in which it is produced. Laid papers have a fine pattern of parallel lines, caused by metal rods in the mould, while wove paper has an almost imperceptible mesh pattern.

SAMPLE SWATCHES
You can obtain swatch books in a variety of colours, textures, and types from paper manufacturers.

WHERE TO BUY PAPER

Art supply shops sell the biggest range of papers, card and mount board. There is no problem with quantity – you can buy as little as one sheet. However, if you want a larger quantity of one type of paper, it may be less expensive to obtain it directly from the paper manufacturer, or from a paper wholesaler. Wholesalers will also supply you with sample swatches free of charge if you request them. These can be very useful for projects that require lots of small pieces in different colours or finishes, such as collage. Another good source for paper is local printers. They buy in quantity for specific jobs and often have paper left over that they will be happy to sell to you. Their prices will be considerably lower than at the art shops, but your choice will be limited and you will probably have to buy a minimum quantity.

PAPER WEIGHT AND SIZE

Paper is sold by weight and different grades of the same type of paper are distinguished by how much a standard quantity of that paper actually weighs. In most of the world, that standard is a sheet of paper 1 metre square, and the weight is measured in terms of grams per square metre (expressed as g/m^2 or gsm).

In the United States, weight is still expressed in pounds and they use the system of basis weights. The standard quantity is a ream, or 500 sheets, but the size of the sheets varies from one category of paper to another. The basis size of bond paper, for example, is 43×56 cm (17×22 in), while the basis size of newsprint is 61×91 cm (24×36 in). Thus, a 50-pound bond paper is actually much heavier than a 50-pound newsprint. The papers in the 'Directory of Papers' are described as light (under 100 gsm), medium (100–180 gsm) and heavy (180–300 gsm).

You need to understand both systems of measurement since you will come across both European-made and American papers.

Paper is available in single sheets.

You can also buy pads in different colours and sizes.

ORIGAMI PAPERS
Available in 30 cm (12 in) and 10 cm (4 in) squares in a range of colours; some have a different colour on the back.

FANCY PAPERS
Printed pattern papers can be very effective for origami.

Directory of Papers

MATERIALS

The type, texture, weight and colour of paper affect suitability for each art form. For example, origami needs a thin paper that can be folded repeatedly without buckling; pop-ups and paper sculptures require robust papers that can stand firmly. The texture and finish of the paper are also important to the appearance of your work. Handmade papers can be hot-pressed, cold-pressed or rough. Hot-pressed paper is fairly smooth, cold-pressed has a slight texture, or 'tooth', and rough paper has a distinct texture. Other treatments, such as coatings, will also affect the surface quality of commercial papers.

Fortunately, despite the apparently complex array of choice, paper can be categorised into the four basic groups listed below:

Uncoated papers comprise the majority of machine-made papers used in the printing industry, many of which are carried by art supply shops and paper distributors. They include white and coloured papers in a range of plain and embossed finishes. Their fibres align in one direction, making folding easy.

Coated papers have highly smooth surfaces on one or both sides and are available in gloss or dull finishes of various brightness. The coloured papers are good for torn sculptural effects or collage, because they reveal an attractive white edge when torn.

Handmade papers are generally produced from cotton or linen rags and used by watercolour and etching artists. They are available from art supply shops and handmade paper suppliers. Their sculptural qualities are superb, because the fibres occur in a random pattern.

Speciality papers include crêpe, tracing and corrugated papers — in fact, all of the papers that fall outside of the other three groups.

Commercial Uncoated

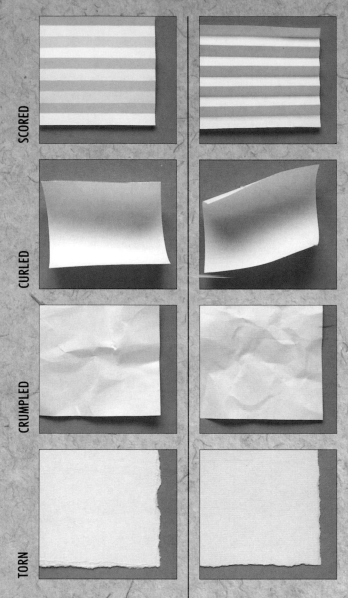

SCORED

CURLED

CRUMPLED

TORN

COVER PAPER
The kind of paper used for booklets and folders. Available in white and a wide range of colours, including bright primaries. Suitable for weaving, collage, paper-cuts, pop-ups, papermaking and paper sculpture. Weight: medium.

BOND PAPER
Everyday paper, available as office and home stationery. Supplied mainly in shades of white, cream and pale grey or blue. Suitable for weaving, collage, paper-cuts, origami, papermaking, papier mâché and paper sculpture. Weight: medium.

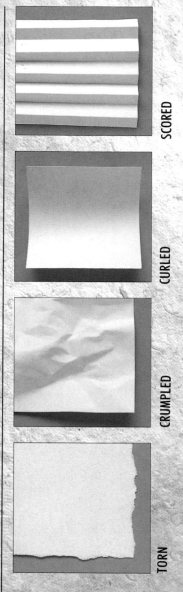
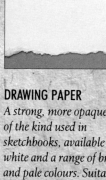

SCORED

CURLED

CRUMPLED

TORN

ART PAPER
Fine paper sold for use by artists, available in various colours. Suitable for weaving, collage, paper-cuts, pop-ups, papermaking and paper sculpture. Weight: white, heavy; colours, medium.

DRAWING PAPER
A strong, more opaque bond of the kind used in sketchbooks, available in white and a range of bright and pale colours. Suitable for collage, pop-ups, papermaking and paper sculpture. Weight: medium.

BRISTOL
Good-quality, fairly heavy paper, ideal for constructional purposes. Supplied in white and various colours. Suitable for collage, pop-ups, papermaking and paper sculpture. Weight: heavy.

RECYCLED
Machine-made recycled papers are available in white and mainly pale colours. Suitable for weaving, collage, paper-cuts, pop-ups, papermaking, papier mâché and paper sculpture. Weight: medium.

Commercial Uncoated: continued

SCORED

CURLED

CRUMPLED

TORN

PARCHMENT
Fine-quality artwork paper available in unusual shades, such as peach and antique gold. Suitable for weaving, collage, paper-cuts, pop-ups, papermaking, papier mâché and paper sculpture. Weight: medium.

KRAFT
Strong, low-cost wrapping paper, ribbed and unbleached. Suitable for weaving, collage, paper-cuts, papermaking, papier mâché and paper sculpture. Weight: medium.

PASTEBOARD
Stiff and relatively thick unlined grey board. Suitable for collage, pop-ups and papermaking. Weight: heavy.

NEWSPRINT
Coarse, weak paper used for newspapers and also sold for rough sketching. Usually white. Suitable for weaving, collage, papercuts, papermaking, papier mâché, and origami. Weight: standard.

Commercial Coated Papers

Handmade Papers

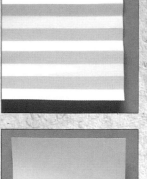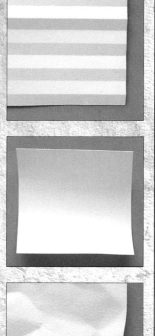

SCORED

CURLED

CRUMPLED

TORN

ART AND PRINTING PAPER
High-quality papers coated in gloss or dull finishes in a variety of colours. Suitable for weaving, collage, paper-cuts, pop-ups and paper sculpture. Weight: heavy.

COVER PAPER
Firm, light, flexible coated card in a wide range of colours. Suitable for weaving, collage, paper-cuts, pop-ups and paper sculpture. Weight: heavy.

HANDMADE RAG LIGHT
Fine-quality, strong, durable white paper, available in cold-pressed, hot-pressed and rough finishes. Suitable for weaving, collage, paper-cuts, papermaking, papier mâché and paper sculpture. Weight: heavy.

HANDMADE RAG HEAVY
A heavier version of light rag paper with the same qualities and availability. Suitable for collage, pop-ups, papermaking and paper sculpture. Weight: heavy.

Handmade Papers: continued

Speciality Papers

SCORED

CURLED

CRUMPLED

TORN

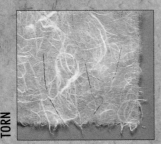

CHINESE HANDMADE
Superior paper suitable for weaving, collage, paper-cuts, papermaking, papier mâché, origami and paper sculpture. Weight: variable.

HANDMADE WITH EMBEDDED OBJECTS
A variety of unusual effects and colours is possible with papers containing embedded items. Suitable for weaving, collage, paper-cuts, papier mâché and paper sculpture. Weight: variable.

CRÊPE
Thin crinkled paper in white and various colours. Suitable for weaving, collage, papermaking and papier mâché. Weight: standard.

TISSUE
Fine, easily crumpled paper, available in white and various colours. Suitable for weaving, collage, papermaking, papier mâché and paper sculpture. Weight: standard.

SCORED

CURLED

CRUMPLED

TORN

TRACING
Highly transparent plain paper with a choice of thickness. Suitable for weaving, collage, origami and paper sculpture. Weight: light and medium.

SUGAR PAPER
Inexpensive, plain paper in a variety of colours. Suitable for collage and weaving. Weight: standard.

CORRUGATED
Light but strong paper traditionally used as packing material for fragile items. Available in natural brown or various colours. Suitable for weaving, collage, pop-ups, papermaking and paper sculpture. Weight: standard.

RICE PAPER
Thin paper made from rice grass, available in natural white. Suitable for weaving, collage, papermaking and papier mâché. Weight: standard.

Tools and Equipment

MATERIALS

Most papercrafts require only basic tools, and you probably already own many of them. Tools for measuring and marking include pencils, rulers, a compass and a triangle. You will also need scissors and knives – or a craft knife with interchangeable blades – for cutting. A cutting mat, although optional, is a good investment, because it saves wear on your knife blades and your work surface. Always use a metal rule or straightedge to guide your knife when cutting a straight line; a plastic ruler is not sturdy enough and could cause the blade to slip and cut you. At best, it will suffer damage itself and become unusable.

You will also want tools and materials to decorate your work, such as paints, pastels, brushes and sprays. More specialised items for occasional use are shown on pages 26–27, but even some of those, or acceptable alternatives, may already be on hand around the house.

More specialised items for occasional use are shown on pages 26–27

BASIC EQUIPMENT CHECK LIST

- ✓ Metal rule
- ✓ Plastic rule
- ✓ Triangle
- ✓ Craft knife
- ✓ Pencils – 2B and 6H
- ✓ Scissors, small and large
- ✓ Cutting mat
- ✓ Paintbrushes
- ✓ Eraser
- ✓ Small wooden skewers

PAINTBRUSHES
2.5 cm (1 in) brush for painting and glazing papier mâché and gluing collage components. Artists' brushes for finer detail.

CUTTING MAT
Self-sealing surface for smooth knife cutting and reduction of wear on blades.

22

KNIVES
A knife with interchangeable blades. You can also use a craft knife with a wedge-shaped blade for cutting straight strips and another with a long fine point for cutting intricate shapes.

TRIANGLE
For drawing straight lines and for use in conjunction with a ruler to draw parallel lines horizontally and vertically.

PENCILS
A 6H for transferring tracings and a 2B for drawing shapes on layout paper.

SMALL WOODEN SKEWERS
For applying small amounts of adhesive, especially useful in paper sculpture.

RULERS
A 30 cm (12 in) plastic ruler for measuring and drawing and a 30 cm (12 in) metal rule for straight-edge cutting.

SCISSORS
Small scissors for detailed pieces and large scissors for cutting out basic shapes.

ERASER
White nylon eraser for removing pencil lines and any other unwanted marks.

Specialised tools

From time to time you will need to use a special piece of equipment: a hole punch to cut circles for eyes, a mould and deckle for papermaking, some polystyrene to build relief effects. These pages show some of the specialised tools that paper artists find most useful, but you can also exploit your ingenuity to discover or improvise an item that works for a particular job. Our alternatives are listed in brackets.

POLYSTYRENE
Available as sheets of different thicknesses, used to elevate the paper layers and create relief effects [corrugated card, polystyrene tiles].

ROLLER
For pressing large pieces of paper onto a background after gluing [rolling pin, dowel].

LARGE SOFT BRUSH
For applying paste to paper [decorators' brush, paste brush].

NEEDLES
For piercing a pattern or making a small connecting hole, for example in mobiles [pins, drawing pins].

PAPERMAKING EQUIPMENT

You must have the following pieces of equipment to make paper: mould and deckle (wooden frames for forming sheets of paper from pulped material); pressing boards (for pressing water out of freshly formed paper); pieces of felt (to layer between freshly made sheets when pressing).

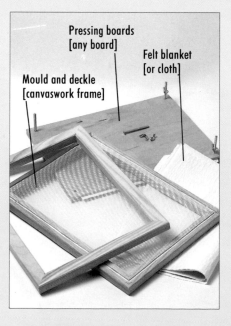

Pressing boards [any board]

Felt blanket [or cloth]

Mould and deckle [canvaswork frame]

24

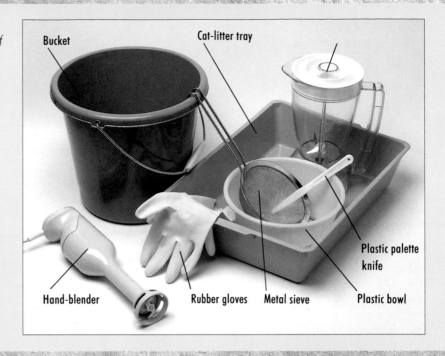

You may be surprised to find that you already have much of the equipment needed, particularly for the papermaking section.

Bucket

Cat-litter tray

Hand-blender

Rubber gloves

Metal sieve

Plastic bowl

Plastic palette knife

STAPLER
For fastening paper instantly. Useful for making quick models of a planned sculpture [paper clips].

WOODEN DOWEL
Used for shaping and curling paper [handle of wooden spoon].

WOODEN SCULPTING TOOLS
For scoring, curling and general shaping [knitting needles, ballpoint pens].

BURNISHER
Ideal for flattening folds [empty ballpoint pen].

HOLE PUNCH/ LEATHER PUNCH
For punching small circles that would be difficult to cut out [paper punch].

WALLPAPER PASTE
Used primarily for papier mâché.

MASKING TAPE
Useful for a variety of purposes, but is more temporary than glue.

Adhesives

A number of strong paper glues are suitable for paper construction. Polyvinyl acetate (PVA) or a quick-bonding all-purpose adhesive is recommended for pop-ups and sculpture, and wallpaper paste or white plastic glue are necessary for papier mâché. Sellotape is useful for temporary fixing.

POLYVINYL ACETATE (PVA)
A good all-purpose adhesive, particularly for paper sculpture and pop-ups.

Finishing

You will often want to add a decorative finish to your art forms. To create a good surface, coat your work with gesso before applying watercolour, acrylic or poster paints.

VARNISH
Make sure you use a clear varnish to seal paper, particularly for découpage.

PAINTS
The most useful paints are watercolour, acrylic and poster paints.

GESSO
Available in tubs and bottles. Used to seal papier mâché before painting.

Mould-Making

To build an original work in papier mâché, you will need materials for making a mould, and a releasing agent to prevent the paper from sticking to it.

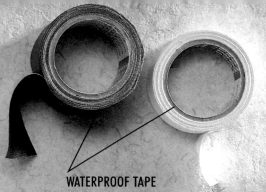
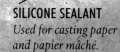

WATERPROOF TAPE
Available in various colours and widths. Used for papermaking and casting.

SILICONE SEALANT
Used for casting paper and papier mâché.

PETROLEUM JELLY
Used for coating casts so that the mould releases easily.

MODELLING CLAY
Used for making models for papier mâché.

FOUND OBJECTS

You can use found objects in a variety of ways for weaving, papier mâché, origami, collage, papermaking and paper sculpture. In addition to the items shown, you can experiment with twigs, leaves, bones, bark, seeds, wallpaper, junk mail, stones, leaflets, wrappers, washers, sand, fabric scraps – to mention just a few!

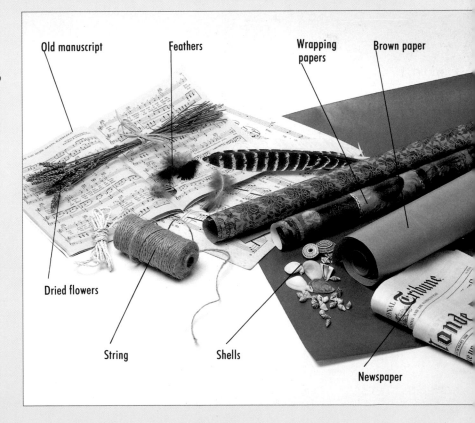

Old manuscript

Feathers

Wrapping papers

Brown paper

Dried flowers

String

Shells

Newspaper

2

Basic Techniques

Folding

BASIC TECHNIQUES

Folding is one of the most elementary techniques of paper art, but there are numerous folds and ways of using them. We have probably all made an aeroplane by folding a piece of paper in half, matching the right side to the left, and creasing the centre fold with our fingers. This is a basic fold, and it must be accurate. If your first fold is incorrect, subsequent folds will be affected, and the finished piece will look wrong. Many of the art forms in this book, such as Pop-Ups, Origami, Weaving and Paper Sculpture, include folding. In this section we show you how to create simple, accurate folds against a straightedge, how to pinch-fold by hand and how to flatten a fold with tools such as a ruler, a roller or a burnisher. Individual folds are shown in the Origami section (see pp. 74–89) and complex shapes are shown in the scoring section (see pp. 38–39).

Before folding paper or cardboard, you should determine the direction of the grain – the alignment of the fibres in the paper. A fold will run smoothly with the grain but crookedly against the grain because the fibres are broken. You can check this by folding your sheet in both directions, but this wastes paper. Instead, bring together opposite edges of the sheet so that it curls; then do the same with the other two edges. You will form a tighter roll one way than the other, and this is the direction of the grain.

There are three ways to flatten a fold – especially important in making pop-ups and some origami forms. On diagrams, folds are indicated by dashed lines.

CREASING BY HAND
Run your thumb firmly along the fold. Repeat with your middle finger nail pushed by your thumb.

USING A RULER
Push the edge of a ruler firmly along the line of the fold. You can also use a burnisher (made of bone or plastic).

USING A ROLLER
Press the fold with an acrylic or rubber roller (available from most art supply shops).

A FOLDED PENGUIN

1 *Take a piece of thin paper 10 cm (4 in) square that is black on one side and white on the other. With the black side facing up, fold diagonally, corner to corner, to form a triangle. Flatten the fold with your fingers.*

2 *Reverse the fold so that the black faces up, and measure 5 cm (2 in) along the fold from the bottom corner. Take the corner and fold it upwards so that the point touches your 5 cm (2 in) mark. Crease the fold with your fingers.*

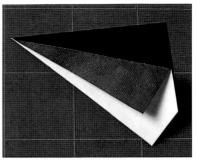

3 *Invert the diagonal fold so that you again have a white triangle with the bottom corner folded up inside the two halves. Bring the top open edge down about 1.3 cm (½ in) from the fold, and crease. Turn over and repeat.*

4 *Place a plastic triangle or ruler diagonally on the paper shape, about 2.5 cm (1 in) from the point. Fold the point upwards, creasing it against the triangle edge. Remove the triangle, fold the point all the way down and crease.*

5 *Half-open the body shape with one hand. Squeeze the point between the finger and thumb of your other hand to reverse the fold and form the head and beak of the penguin.*

6 *Check that both sides are perfectly even. Then flatten the fold you have just created with your forefinger.*

7 *Fold the penguin completely flat and press all folds again between your forefingers and thumbs.*

8 *Carefully open the centre fold to reveal the penguin. Pull the wings slightly away from the body.*

9 *The finished penguin should show crisp folds and stand up straight.*

Crumpling

Irregular creases can be used to form a 3-D structure, surface texture, and to enhance a background or a sculptural component. Bear in mind that crumpling greatly reduces the size of the paper. To build a 3-D structure, tightly crumple a flat sheet, then open it and model it into the desired shape. The creases allow you to shape the paper in virtually any direction, and by gathering, pleating and pinching you can achieve some stunning abstract shapes. Another method is to begin with a regular geometric form, such as a cube, cylinder or pyramid, and then completely crumple it. Reopen the form and carefully pull some of the wrinkles out from the crumpled surface to create a more organic, naturalistic version of the original shape. Crumpled paper can also provide a softening contrast with regular textures. Lightweight papers are best for crumpling — usually the thinner the paper, the more successful the crumpled forms.

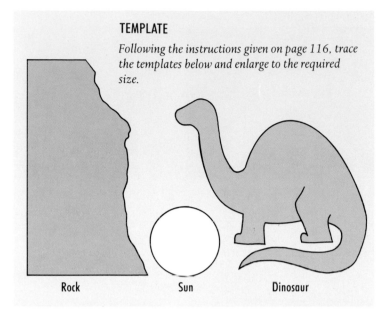

TEMPLATE

Following the instructions given on page 116, trace the templates below and enlarge to the required size.

Rock   Sun   Dinosaur

Crumpling effects depend upon the paper used. Bond papers, such as most everyday stationery, allow sharp but light creases, whereas heavier cover papers give more pronounced effects. Cotton rag paper has no grain – its fibres are randomly distributed – so it can be modelled into soft creases. Layout paper, used by graphic artists to try out their ideas, is extremely light and malleable, but tracing paper is too brittle; the creases appear white and can split. Metallic or shiny papers reflect the light and can add interesting facets.

METALLIC PAPER

Light-reflecting, adding facets to crumpled work.

RAG PAPER

Gives soft creases, resists tearing, easy to paint.

LAYOUT PAPER

Light, translucent and excellent for crumpling.

BOND PAPER

Fairly light; crumples in sharp surface wrinkles.

COVER PAPER

Varied colours; gives heavy, lasting creases.

TRACING PAPER

Thin, transparent but too brittle to crumple.

A CRUMPLED DINOSAUR

1 On a piece of grey, medium- to lightweight paper, draw around the template using a black fineline marker. This will ensure that your outline is visible after you have crumpled the paper. Roll the paper into a crumpled ball.

2 Carefully unravel the ball of paper to avoid tearing it (you will notice that crumpling softens the paper), and with a small pair of scissors cut around the black outline.

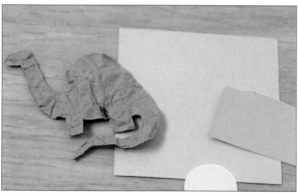

3 Cut out a 10 cm (4 in) piece of thin card for the sky and a green rectangle with a torn top edge for the grass. Next draw a mountain shape on a piece of stone-coloured paper and tear along the outline. Crumple all these pieces to add texture.

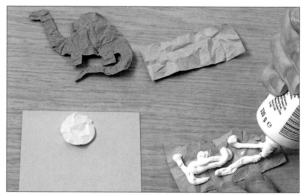

4 Apply a layer of silicone bathtub sealant to the reverse of the sun shape. This will be used on each component to act as an adhesive and as a support. Place the sun on the blue card, pressing gently to fix it at the desired level.

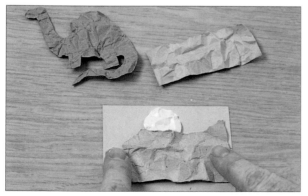

5 Coat the back of each piece in turn with silicone sealant, working from the background to the foreground, adjusting the levels as necessary.

6 Finally, apply the sealant to the dinosaur and fix it in position. Set the finished piece aside for several hours to enable the sealant to dry.

Curling

**BASIC
TECHNIQUES**

Different methods of curling paper reveal how light affects the surface of a work and gives it added dimension.

Identify and then follow the direction of the grain (see p. 36) where possible in order to manipulate the paper smoothly. Curl the paper by rolling it in your hands, or pull it over the straight edge of a table or over a scissors blade. Wind it around a wooden dowel or tightly around a small wooden skewer. Roll it tighter than you need it, because it always springs open slightly. When curling components — in paper sculpture, for example — cut them out before shaping them. You can tighten a curl by rewinding.

TIPS FOR USING CURLED PAPER

✓ Pinch or crease basic curled shapes, such as coils, scrolls and S-shapes, into hearts, triangles and V-shapes.

✓ Use curled paper to decorate a greetings card with a seasonal motif such as a candle.

✓ Cover the lid and side of a box with a pattern of curled shapes. Dense coils can make a strong surface that will not crush.

✓ Create a scene with curled forms, using strips of different widths to vary the relief. Craft shops carry ready-cut strips.

✓ Apply curled forms to an object by gluing the centre of each shape and placing it in position. Tweezers or a toothpick will be a help.

✓ Try spraying a design with paint or varnish.

The method you use to curl paper will vary, depending on the length of the strip, the type of paper and the effect required. In general, for small, tight curls use pressure or a small stick and for looser curls, relax the pressure or use a larger stick.

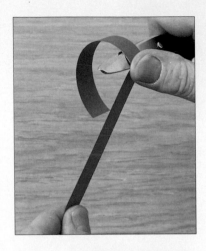

USING A SCISSORS BLADE
Curl cut-out components by pulling them against the scissors blade. Use your thumb to apply pressure. The harder you press, the tighter the end will be. Be careful, however, not to pull too hard, or the paper will tear.

TIGHTER CURLS
Use a small wooden skewer in the same way as the scissors, or roll the paper around it to achieve a tight curl. This works especially well with small pieces.

HAND PULLING
Keeping one hand on the paper while pulling it down over the edge of a table with the other is a good method for large strips.

A CURLED SNAIL

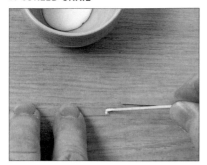

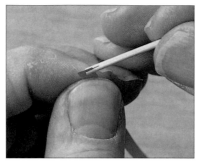

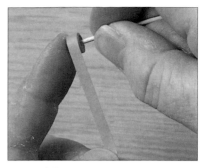

1 Cut a strip of lightweight orange paper 3–6 mm (⅛–¼ in) wide and about 51 cm (20 in) long. You can join pieces by overlapping them by 3 mm (⅛ in) and attaching them with glue.

2 With a sharp craft knife, cut the tip off a wooden skewer and make a small slit in its place. Slide one end of the orange paper strip into the slit but do not let it protrude to the other side.

3 Coil the strip around the skewer in one revolution, and where the paper touches to complete the first layer apply glue. Continue to coil the strip evenly around the skewer until the end.

4 Take the coil off the skewer and form an eccentric coil. Tweezers are useful for holding the coil.

5 Holding the coil in place, apply a small dab of glue across all the layers to maintain the eccentric shape. Set aside until the glue dries.

6 Using a 25 cm (10 in) strip of green paper, repeat steps 4 and 5 on both sides to form a long thin oval. When set, pinch one end to a point.

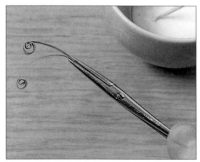

9 Apply several dabs of glue to the underside of the eyes and position them on the head to complete your snail.

7 To make the eyes, coil green paper around the skewer 2½ times. Secure it with glue. Repeat, and attach eyes at the base of the stems. Hold the coils together with tweezers.

8 Holding the shell and body with tweezers, apply tiny dots of glue to the undersides. Position them on a piece of card. Press them gently in place with your finger.

Tearing

BASIC TECHNIQUES

Tearing offers a contrast to the hard edge of scissor- or knife-cuts and reveals the structure of the paper. You can tear paper as shown right or, if you want a straight edge, you can draw a line, place a ruler with its edge on the line and tear upwards, away from the ruler and towards yourself. Tear with the grain if you want a straight line, or against the grain if you want an irregular look.

White paper coated with colour will tear to reveal a white edge. Use a flash of white outline here and there to accentuate the colour and give your work impact. You can control the amount of white by the way you tear the paper. Tearing away from yourself, coloured side up, rips the paper on the reverse side and almost eliminates the white. Tearing towards you gives a distinct white edge.

Hold and tear the paper in the way that feels most comfortable. A right-handed person, for example, will probably hold paper in the left hand, with thumb on top and forefinger underneath, tearing downwards against the nail of the forefinger.

Tearing shapes for sculpture and collage needs additional control. Score the shapes first with a stylus (see p. 22), being careful not to cut through the paper. You can then tear out the shape.

WITH THE GRAIN

AGAINST THE GRAIN

To test for the grain, hold two adjacent edges of the sheet and bend it in half. Then take the other two edges and bend in half again. It is easier to bend with the grain than against it. This is true of all papers, although it is easier to see with a thicker paper.

WITH THE GRAIN

AGAINST THE GRAIN

Tearing with the grain gives a smooth line that follows the fibres of the paper. Tearing against the grain creates a ragged effect because it breaks the fibres.

TEMPLATES
Following the instructions given on page 116, trace the templates below and enlarge to the required size.

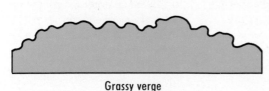

Grassy verge

Wool　　　　　　　　**Body**

A TORN SHEEP

1 *Trace the sheep's fleece template and transfer it onto a piece of medium-weight cream-coloured paper. Then draw over the outline with a pointed stylus. This creates a groove of weakened fibres that help control your tearing. As you pull the paper apart, they will be the first to tear.*

2 *Cut around the fleece shape, leaving a margin of about 2.5 cm (1 in) all round. Hold the shape carefully in one hand moving your thumb along the drawn line as you slowly tear around the image with the other. Pull the paper upwards, against the thumb of your holding hand.*

3 *When you have torn all around the shape, neaten the edges by pinching away uneven bits of paper with your fingers or a pair of tweezers.*

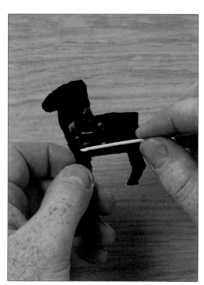

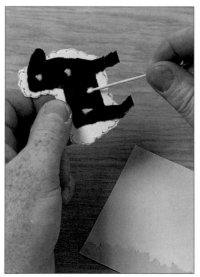

4 *Repeat steps 1 to 3 on the black body and on the grass. The fine tips of grass will need extra care. When all the pieces are torn, use a toothpick to dab a few drops of glue on the black body, and attach it to the back of the fleece.*

5 *Cut out a 10 cm (4 in) square of pale blue paper and glue the grass strip to one edge. Dot some glue on the back of the completed sheep and attach it to the background, pressing firmly with your hand to flatten the image.*

6 *The torn ragged edges suggest the soft fleecy outline of wool far more effectively than a cleanly cut edge.*

Scoring

Scoring is used extensively in cardboard constructions, such as pop-ups and packaging, and is fundamental to paper sculpture. It enables you to create relief or build intricate pop-up mechanisms. Scoring also lends rigidity; the scored line acts like a spine to strengthen your creations.

There are two main types of scoring tool. The first is a stylus, or blunt-tipped instrument, which is pushed into the paper and pulled along a ruler or straightedge. The paper is then bent away from the indented line to create a well-defined, uniform fold. The second is a knife, used to cut a groove into the paper to weaken the area you want to fold. Practise this until you feel confident about the pressure required: if you press too hard, you will cut through the paper, and if you are too gentle, the fold will not be smooth. This method allows you to create curves that

appear to defy the limits of paper construction (see Paper Sculpture pp. 152–171). Our project shows you how to make a turtle, using both types of scoring tool. The shell is composed of multiple curved scores on a single piece of yellow-green medium-weight paper.

Experiment with different papers, cards and shapes, and make a note of interesting discoveries so that you can incorporate them into future work. Keep some samples as a visual record and you could build an exciting collection of geometric and organic shapes.

TEMPLATES
Following the instructions given on page 116, trace the templates below and enlarge to the required size.

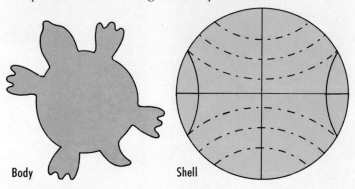

Body

Shell

The purpose of scoring is to create a fault in the paper along which it will bend. There are several ways of achieving this.

INCISING

Run a craft knife lightly across the surface of the paper to carve a shallow incision. Bend the paper away from the cut.

PIERCING

Use the pointed tip of a craft knife to pierce a series of cuts in the paper. The thicker the paper, the closer the cuts should be.

BURNISHING

With a blunt stylus or a bone burnisher, score firmly along the paper and bend away from the score.

A SCORED TURTLE

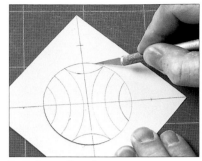

1 *Rule two lines from corner to corner of a 12.5 cm (5 in) square. Taking their intersection as your centre, use a compass to draw a circle 10 cm (4 in) in diameter. Trace and transfer the fold lines from the shell template.*

2 *Cut out the circle. Score lightly with the tip of a craft knife on the inside and outside of all the curves except the two middle ones. These will lie at the head and tail of the turtle. Be careful not to cut through the paper.*

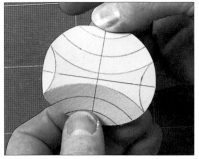

3 *Bend the paper away from the incised line to form a mountain fold (see p.53). Make sure that the entire curve folds back evenly by running your finger and thumb around it. Repeat this procedure on all the scored curves.*

4 *Score the remaining two curves with a blunt stylus. Turn the shell over. Define the indentations more clearly by bending the paper away from them. You now have one mountain fold and two valley folds in each side of the shell.*

5 *To make the two mountain folds as crisp as the valley folds, score the indented lines with a craft knife just enough to make a small incision in the paper. Turn over and score the two remaining curves top and bottom.*

6 *Bend paper away from the top and bottom scored curves, holding the sides between your fingers and thumbs as shown. Push the sides towards each other slightly to form the finished shell.*

7 *Trace the body template, transfer it to a piece of brown medium-weight paper and cut it out. Score all the lines from the back with a blunt stylus. The tail will form a mountain fold and the flippers will show indentations.*

8 *Put two dabs of glue on the underside of the shell in the middle of the mountain folds. Turn the shell over and place it on top of the body. Press the glue points with the blunt stylus until they adhere firmly.*

9 *The finished turtle gains its dimension from the variety of incised and indented lines.*

Embossing

BASIC TECHNIQUES

Embossing is the technique of adding relief to paper by burnishing with a stylus or a round-tipped tool over a raised shape, such as a cardboard cutout. You can see many examples of embossing on greetings cards, expensive letterheads, invitations and book covers.

In the printing industry, there are several different embossing terms: a blind emboss, a printed emboss and a multi-level emboss. A blind emboss is an embossed image on a plain piece of paper without the use of a printed image. For a printed emboss, the image is first printed on the paper and then embossed with a simple raised shape on one level. This treatment gives the printed image an added dimension. The multi-level emboss is just that – an embossed image with varying levels. This is the most expensive form of embossing since it requires hand-made metal dies.

Using variations of these methods, you can create delightful embossed images of your own with a minimum of equipment. By following the step-by-step demonstration of the dolphin you will see how easy and effective embossing is. Try experimenting with thicker and thinner card shapes and gluing together different levels of card to create your own multi-level emboss. The important thing to remember is to keep most of your corners slightly rounded as it is difficult to get the burnishing tool into sharp corners. Watercolour papers made of 100 per cent cotton rag are the best to use, as they will withstand more handling.

TEMPLATES
Following the instructions given on page 116, trace the template and enlarge to the required size.

WET AND DRY EMBOSSING

You can obtain satisfactory results with dry embossing, and you will not have to wait for it to dry. However, you will find that you can push the paper to greater limits when you dampen it first.

DRY PAPER

As the stylus marks clearly show, you will need to press harder with dry paper. But take care not to tear the paper.

DAMP PAPER

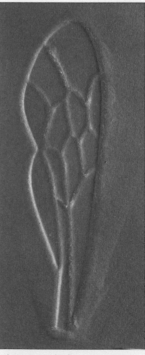

This example demonstrates the greater detail possible when you dampen the paper – the lines of the fin are sharper.

AN EMBOSSED DOLPHIN

1 Transfer the tracing of the template onto a piece of medium-weight card 15 cm (6 in) square. Use a sharp blade to cut out the background outline, including the internal form of the dolphin and the water droplets.

2 Glue the cut-out background to another 15 cm (6 in) square of card. This will act as a base to hold all the cut-outs together. Paste the two halves of the dolphin into place on the base.

3 Measure and draw a 10 cm (4 in) square around your assembled embossing jig to enable you to position your paper accurately on top of it.

4 Immerse a 10 cm (4 in) square of blue medium-weight paper in a tray of water.

5 Blot excess moisture with kitchen paper, leaving the sheet damp and flexible. Store additional squares between moist pieces of kitchen paper if you want to make several impressions of the same emboss.

6 Align the damp sheet carefully on the pencilled square. Because it is wet you can't tape it in position, so hold it firmly while embossing.

7 Using a round-ball burnishing tool, gently rub the paper into the cut-out shape. Work cautiously to sense the correct degree or pressure: too much and the paper will tear; too little and the embossed line will be ill-defined.

8 When you can see the image clearly in negative (from the back), carefully peel away the paper from the top, keeping your other hand on the opposite bottom corner.

9 The finished boss should look like this, with distinct, well-formed, swelling lines. The cardboard jig can be reused several times.

Cutting

Good cutting can make the difference between a well-finished piece of work and a jagged, untidy one – as anyone who has cut out a circle freehand will know. The two tools for cutting paper are scissors and craft knives. Both have their merits for particular tasks, but generally you should choose whichever you feel more comfortable using.

There are numerous hobby or craft knives, but the best choice is the type with a choice of handles to which you can fit a range of interchangeable blades, such as the Stanley knife. Blades should include the long, sharp, finely pointed frisket blade, designed for clean cutting without pressure, and a mount blade for sturdier work. A round handle is preferable to a flat-sided one, as rolling it in your fingers as you cut can make it easier to achieve flowing curves. You will also need three pairs of scissors: a 20 cm (8 in) pair, a 10 cm (4 in) pair and some small needlework scissors for fine detail. It is easier to make accurate

TEMPLATE
Following the instructions given on page 116, trace the template and enlarge to the required size.

scissor cuts by keeping the scissors fixed in one hand and feeding the work through them with the other hand. Scissors will not cut through materials heavier than medium-weight paper and lightweight card, however; for these you must use a scalpel or a craft knife fitted with the appropriate blade.

Hold the knife as if it were a pen. This gives you greater control. Practise rolling the handle as you cut, so that you are not limited by the movement of your wrists when cutting a tight curve. In cutting, practice makes perfect.

SCISSORS

Keep the scissors still and turn the paper into the path of the blades. This method produces more accurate cuts than keeping the paper still and moving the scissors.

KNIFE

A sharp blade always gives a crisp edge. With a little practice you will find it as comfortable as using a pencil, enabling you to make flowing curves. Use a cutting mat to save wear on your blade and damage to furniture.

A CUTOUT ZEBRA

1 Draw the zebra directly onto white paper 10 cm (4 in) square, or transfer the template so that it appears in reverse (facing right). That way there will be no pencil marks to erase when you turn your cutout over.

2 Begin cutting out the traced shapes, keeping all the lines crisp and flowing. Cut completely into corners, so that the shapes drop out neatly.

3 To cut a thin pointed shape, work downwards from both sides to meet at the point. This avoids pulling at the fine detail, which could cause creasing.

4 You can then lift the shape out with the tip of your knife blade.

5 Continue cutting until you have completed the zebra head.

6 Take a 10 cm (4 in) square of black paper to serve as your background. Apply dots of glue to the underside of the cut-out with a toothpick.

7 Place the cut-out sheet over the black paper, lining up the left-hand side and the top. When it is accurately positioned, press it with your hand or flatten it with a roller. Allow the glue to dry.

8 At the end of step 5, you were left with a small piece that was not connected to the rest of the head. Use it to form the bottom right corner. Glue it into position and press it down with your finger.

9 The finished head should be a crisp, clear image, with no glue visible on the black paper.

43

Piercing

Piercing is a means of creating surface texture. A variety of tools can be used, including pins, knives, punches, tracing wheels, knitting needles and a stylus. The only limit to your options is your imagination.

You can create an entire design by piercing or use it as a partial effect. Geometric designs are easy to make with the aid of squared paper. Draw a pattern of dots at the intersections of the squares on a sheet of graph paper. Place the sheet over a piece of coloured paper, attach the two to a polystyrene board and push pins through your design. Polystyrene is the best support for all piercing methods, because sharp points sink easily into it, ensuring a clean cut, without damaging your work surface. Incised patterns can be raised from the paper to give added texture to designs and backgrounds, or greater realism to features such as feathers and scales. Make your own reference file of textures by using a variety of piercing tools on a white sheet of watercolour paper. Label each mark to identify the tool that made it. Experiment with different effects.

TEMPLATES
Following the instructions given on pages 116–7, trace the templates and enlarge to the required size.

Head

Body

Tail

Anything that you can push through paper can be used to add texture – from nails and knitting needles for rough marks to pins and knives for fine holes and slits.

You will find it easier to work with a needle if you push a small cork over the blunt end. Place paper on a piece of polystyrene board.

SMALL HOLES
Piercing with needles of different thicknesses produces the effect of a dot-screen picture as seen in newspapers. The closer the dots, the blacker the area, and vice versa.

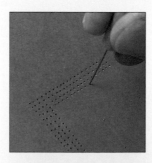

LARGER HOLES
Larger holes can be achieved with numerous tools, such as a blunt stylus, an awl, dried-up ballpoint pens, nails, knitting needles or sharpened wooden dowels.

CRAFT KNIFE PIERCING
A pointed craft knife blade gives a thin vertical wedge shape. This can be used in a series of alternating rows to create unusual patterns.

PUNCHING
Leather punches create interesting borders, but you are limited to the edge of the paper by the maximum opening of the punch.

A PIERCED FISH

1 *Transfer the traced image of the round body part onto a piece of red paper and make the V-shaped cuts with a sharp craft knife. Be careful not to over-cut near the edge of the paper or you will weaken the shape.*

2 *Hold the edges between fingers and thumbs and curl the paper back. The V-shapes pop out to form raised scales.*

3 *From the back, pierce alternate scales with a needle, making a triangle of six holes (three, two and one). Apply knife slits to the remaining scales, forming a triangle of three slits on each.*

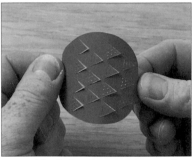

4 *Curl back the edges again to see the effect of this patterning.*

5 *Transfer the tracing of the fins and tail assembly onto orange paper. Pierce needle holes along the lines of the tail, and a hole at the end of each fin line. Cut from these holes to the end of each pierced line with a craft knife.*

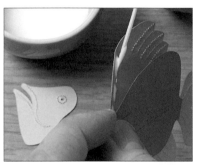

6 *Using a toothpick, apply a line of glue along the edges of the orange part. Place the red section on top, curving slightly so that scales protrude. Cut out the head, pierce its detail with a needle and glue it into position.*

7 *On a piece of 10 cm (4 in) square pale blue paper, pierce bubble shapes of varying size with a needle. Create a shadow on one side of each bubble by piercing three rows of holes.*

8 *Put two dabs of glue on the reverse of the fish, one at the front of the head and one at the base of the tail. Glue the fish to the blue square, leaving a slight curl in the middle so that it retains shape. Lift some scales with a knife.*

9 *The completed fish gains its effect from a variety of pierced patterns that are accentuated by light and shadow.*

Colouring

BASIC TECHNIQUES

The advantage of colouring paper yourself is that you can achieve exactly the shade or effect that you want. You can do this by brush-painting, sponging, spattering, colour washing and marbling.

Sponging works best with watercolour paper, a natural sponge and the vinyl paints used in producing animated films. If you cannot find these, use artist's acrylics.

Spattering mottles the paper surface, giving visual weight to the work. Marbling can create rich and original patterns. You can use aerosol paints, oil paint diluted with turpentine or drawing inks (see opposite).

TEMPLATES

Following the instructions given on page 116, trace the templates and enlarge to the required size.

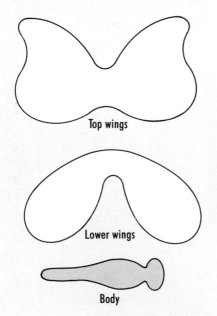

Top wings

Lower wings

Body

Often you need a specific colour to complete a project. If you can't find the right ready-mixed shade, the only answer is to colour the paper yourself. You can do this in several ways: brush-painting, sponging, spattering, colour-washing and marbling (see opposite).

BRUSH-PAINTING

When using a special colour for a component – in a paper sculpture, for example – cut the piece from white paper before painting with acrylic or watercolour. That way you can colour the edges.

SPONGING

Mix paint to a light creamy consistency and dip a sponge into it. Dab the excess onto a piece of newspaper until you see the texture and depth of colour that you want. Apply the sponge to your paper in random dabs.

SPATTERING

Spattering gives a project texture, and is similar to a coarse airbrush effect. Load a toothbrush with colour and point it downwards towards the paper. Draw a piece of stiff card towards you over the bristles, so that paint flicks onto the paper.

COLOUR WASHES

For successful colour washes, wet the paper first and stretch it on a wooden board, holding it down with gummed paper tape. Allow the paper to dry thoroughly before washing colour over it with a wide watercolour brush.

A MARBLED BUTTERFLY

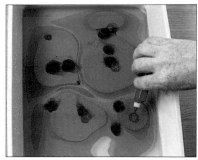

1 *Half-fill a tray with water. Scatter the surface with a few random drops of waterproof blue ink. As they begin to spread, add some drops of red.*

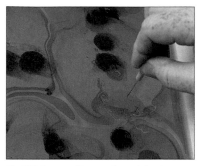

2 *With a needle, gently swirl one colour into the other. The movements of your needle are reflected in the pattern of the inks. Try clockwise and anti-clockwise actions until you are happy with the result.*

3 *Hold a piece of watercolour paper by diagonally opposite corners. Keeping hold of the corners, lower a free corner onto the water surface, followed in one smooth movement by the rest of the paper.*

4 *As soon as the paper touches the surface, begin lifting it off in reverse order, picking up the opposite corner first and peeling away. Turn the sheet over. If necessary, repeat the process.*

5 *Trace the butterfly template onto a piece of scrap paper and cut it out to make a template of your own. This can be moved around over the marbled pattern until you find an area you like for the butterfly wings.*

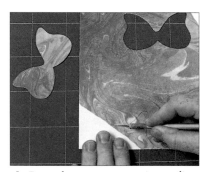

6 *Draw the two separate wing outlines on the marbled paper and cut them out with a craft knife. Save the spare paper for another project.*

7 *Cut the butterfly body out of grey paper and spatter it with blue ink. Score a line down the centre and fold it in half to form a V. Then score a line down the centre of each wing and fold forwards in a slight V shape.*

8 *Glue the two sets of wings into position along the score line. Use a toothpick to put a dot of glue on each side of the body's underside and attach it to the top of the wing assembly.*

9 *The finished butterfly. Try the same project with a different pair of colouring techniques.*

Menagerie Sampler

BASIC TECHNIQUES

At this point in the book you should possess nine splendid animal motifs covering all the basic techniques. It would be a pity to leave them on a shelf collecting dust or to hide them away in a drawer, so why not display them in a shadow box frame as a reminder of the techniques? This display frame design can be adapted for all the projects in the book. If you are a confident woodworker, you can construct a simple wooden frame with nine divisions. Alternatively, you could ask a professional picture framer to make one for you.

Here we show you how to make a basic polystyrene box. Simply follow the step-by-step instructions and add a finish of your choice. When gluing the animals to the backing board, first glue small blocks of polystyrene to the back of each. When your menagerie is complete, hang the framed work in a place of honour. Remember not to expose it to direct sunlight as the paper colours will fade.

DISPLAYING YOUR MENAGERIE

When arranging your creatures in the frame, you need to consider colour, lighting, shapes and textures. Some will require a background, others will need to be raised with 1.3 cm (½ in) polystyrene blocking.

A CUTOUT ZEBRA

Cutting, pages 42–3
A layer of polystyrene flat against the back raises the zebra slightly.

A SCORED TURTLE

Scoring, pages 38–9
An earthy-textured backing paper complements the colours of the snail. With a dab of glue attach a small oblong piece of polystyrene to raise the turtle above the background. This will give more interesting shadow and depth.

A TORN SHEEP

Tearing, pages 36–7
The sheep is raised slightly by inserting a backing of thin polystyrene.

MAKING THE BOX

1 *Cut four strips of polystyrene 5 x 32 cm (2 x 12½ in). Make two 0.6 x 3.2 cm (¼ x 1¼ in) slits in each piece 10 cm (4 in) from each end.*

2 *Slot the four pieces together to make nine square divisions. Add glue to the bottom edge of each and press down on a 33 x 33 cm (13 x 13 in) polystyrene base.*

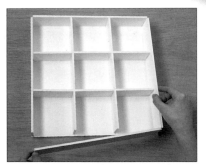

3 *Cut two pieces of 7.5 x 66 cm (3 x 26 in) polystyrene. Score lightly with a craft knife half way along each strip. Bend them in half. Glue the two right-angled pieces to the base to form walls.*

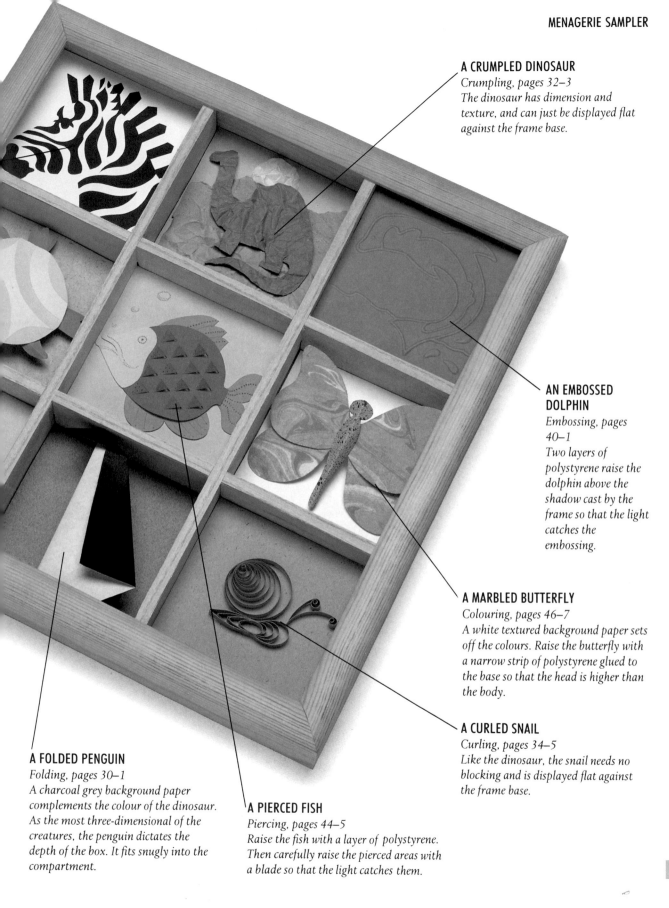

A CRUMPLED DINOSAUR
Crumpling, pages 32–3
The dinosaur has dimension and texture, and can just be displayed flat against the frame base.

AN EMBOSSED DOLPHIN
Embossing, pages 40–1
Two layers of polystyrene raise the dolphin above the shadow cast by the frame so that the light catches the embossing.

A MARBLED BUTTERFLY
Colouring, pages 46–7
A white textured background paper sets off the colours. Raise the butterfly with a narrow strip of polystyrene glued to the base so that the head is higher than the body.

A CURLED SNAIL
Curling, pages 34–5
Like the dinosaur, the snail needs no blocking and is displayed flat against the frame base.

A FOLDED PENGUIN
Folding, pages 30–1
A charcoal grey background paper complements the colour of the dinosaur. As the most three-dimensional of the creatures, the penguin dictates the depth of the box. It fits snugly into the compartment.

A PIERCED FISH
Piercing, pages 44–5
Raise the fish with a layer of polystyrene. Then carefully raise the pierced areas with a blade so that the light catches them.

3

Art Forms

Pop-ups

Most of us remember childhood books whose stories were brought to life with wonderful pop-up pictures. Today, many of us receive greetings cards whose message pops up when the card opens. Some are so ingenious that you want to go on playing with them and discover how they are constructed.

There are ten basic mechanisms for pop-ups, and these act as a starting point for all the variations found in books and cards. Using these mechanisms you can create images that spring up, slide, rotate and move in a variety of ways. Here we show you how to make single slit, double-slit in two variations, multi-slit, pull-up planes, moving arm, V-fold and dissolving scenes. The remaining three mechanisms (magic box, rotating disk and pivoting motion) are complicated and are best tried only after you are thoroughly familiar with the ones in this book.

It is especially important when constructing pop-ups to make sure that your measurements, scores, cuts and folds are accurate, or the mechanism will not work. Use a triangle, ruler and protractor to keep scoring straight and square. It helps to make one or two roughs before attempting your finished design.

Whenever you see a pop-up mechanism that you find interesting and may want to use at a later date, make some notes or a rough copy of it and file it for reference.

TOOLS AND MATERIALS

- ✓ Metal ruler
- ✓ Protractor
- ✓ Triangle
- ✓ Craft knife
- ✓ Pencil
- ✓ Glue
- ✓ Scissors
- ✓ Cutting mat
- ✓ Scoring stylus
- ✓ Eraser
- ✓ Clear tape
- ✓ Medium- and lightweight card
- ✓ Medium- and heavyweight paper

COMBINING TECHNIQUES

This pop-up is a mix of several mechanisms. The ingenious design of the lips resembles that of a rose and produces a striking image overall (Annèe Galtier).

A V-FOLD POP-UP

The artist used extensive decoration around the main mechanism to great effect. This composition explodes with life and colour (Theresa Pindroh).

SIMPLE COMPLEXITY

The success of this card is based on meticulous measurement. Cut from a simple rectangle and creased with a bone folder, the mechanism moves forwards and backwards (Paul Jackson).

POP-UP TECHNIQUES

CUT LINES

Cuts are indicated by a continuous line. Use a knife for pop-ups, making sure that you start at the beginning of the line and finish at the end.

VALLEY FOLDS

A valley fold is folded upwards. These folds are shown by a broken line.

MOUNTAIN FOLDS

A mountain fold folds back to form a peak. These folds are indicated by a line of dashes and dots.

Single Slit

The single-slit mechanism is composed of a series of valley and mountain folds. It works across the centre fold of the card, turning part of it from a valley fold into a mountain fold. This is the basis for several pop-up effects. The slit can be any shape and begin anywhere on the central fold provided the end of it is connected to the central fold by a scored fold.

1 *Fold a piece of card in half and make a horizontal cut from the fold halfway across the sheet, making sure that you cut through both layers of card.*

2 *Score a diagonal line from the fold to the end of the cut line. Do the same above the cut line.*

3 *Fold both scored lines forwards to form a V. Flatten the folds with your thumbs, then fold them down again so that the cut lines meet.*

4 *Turn the card over and repeat step 3, folding both scored lines firmly back the other way, and then flat again.*

5 *Opening up the card, you will have one cut line and four scored lines forming a diamond pattern across the centre fold.*

6 *Holding the bottom of the card, pull the top part of the diamond forwards from the cut line to fold inwards. Repeat with the bottom half of the diamond. Then close the card.*

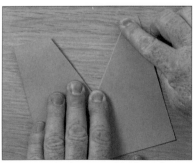

7 *Flatten both inverted folds with your forefinger to establish their direction.*

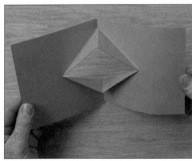

8 *Opening and closing the card will cause the diamond shape to work in reverse. It will open as you close the card, and close when you open it. This is also the basis for the moving arm.*

Double Slit – Symmetrical

This technique is similar to the one used for single slit (left) but allows for greater creative scope. Basically it always has two slits in the central fold. These can be any shape and are connected by a fold. This fold does not have to be parallel to the central crease.

1 Fold a rectangular piece of card in half. With the fold to the left, make two horizontal slits through both thicknesses of the card from the fold to half-way across the card. Fold the centre flap to the left as shown.

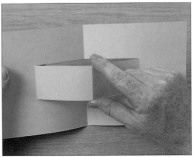

2 Fold the flap back again and open the card. Pull the central flap forwards from the fold. Close the card, pressing the front with your hand. When you open and close the card the flap will open and close in the opposite direction.

Double Slit – Asymmetrical

The pop-ups shown so far spring symmetrically from a central fold. This variation of the double slit pops up to one side, or asymmetrically. Instead of working through both folded halves of the card at the same time, we must now work on the unfolded card and measure the construction lines precisely to achieve a smooth mechanism.

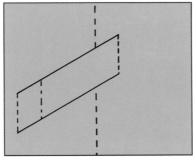

1 On some card 21.5 × 28 cm (8½ x 11 in) lightly draw the lines as shown. Make sure that measurements are accurate. You will end up with four valley folds, one mountain fold and two parallel cut lines.

2 Check that all the lines on the mechanism are parallel. Then, with a craft knife and metal rule, cut along the full length of both cut lines.

3 Using your scoring stylus, score the two valley folds along the central strip, and the one mountain fold. Then score either side of the slit section and the two central valley folds.

4 Hold the card up and close it slightly as you pull the mountain fold forwards between the cut-out section.

5 Pinch the valley folds at each end of the slit section to flatten them. Close the card, making sure that the mountain fold comes forwards as you do so. Then flatten all folds on the closed card.

Multi-slit – Asymmetrical

This multi-slit is simply a pair of double-slit pop-ups of diminishing size. It is possible to make a continuing series by adding more pairs of slits, which in turn will create more mountain and valley folds. But the more folds you create, the harder the card will be to open and close.

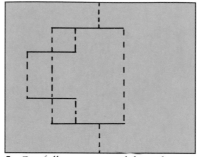

1 Carefully measure and draw the above configuration on any piece of card. Number the slits 1 to 4 to save confusion. You will end up with a stepped pop-up of three mountain folds and six valley folds.

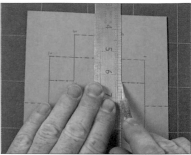

2 Cut the four slits, using a craft knife and a metal rule: from 1–1, 2–2, 3–3, 4–4. Keep all cuts straight and parallel. Score all the fold lines with a stylus along a ruler. Be careful not to score through the centre fold.

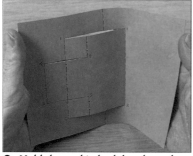

3 Hold the card in both hands, and close it slightly while pushing the valley fold 1–2 from behind to establish the longest fold.

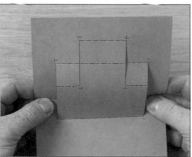

4 Holding the end at right angles, pull the three mountain folds forward and up, so that the pop-up step is at 90° to the card.

5 Close the card and flatten all folds from the back with your thumb to establish the finished pop-up.

6 Open the card to test the mechanism. When the card is opened at 90°, all folds should be correspondingly at 90° and form three neat steps.

MULTI-SLIP POP-UP

The multi-slit mechanism is useful because it makes a good foundation for more complex pop-up shapes. When attaching a shaped piece to the mechanism, open the card so that the two halves are at right angles, then you will clearly see where to seat the base of the piece you are sticking on; otherwise you will end up with a gap at the bottom.

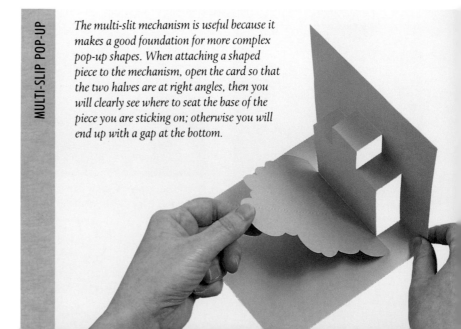

Pull-up Planes

This device is often used in pop-up books to reveal a hidden image. It works on the lever principle. Pulling the paper tab at the bottom causes a flap of paper to lift up as a fold pulls against the top slot.

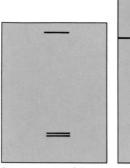
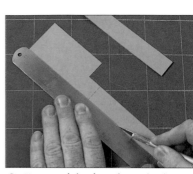

1 *Measure and draw on a piece of card the artwork shown above.*

2 *Use a craft knife and metal rule to cut out the pop-up flap and pull tab.*

3 *Run a metal stylus along the fold line a couple of times to establish a definite score.*

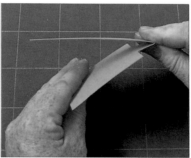

4 *Holding the pop-up flap in one hand, bend the tab along the scored line and flatten the fold.*

5 *Take the second piece of card, which will form the base. Cut out the slot at the top. Then cut the slit for the tab to return through. Finally make the cut at the bottom.*

6 *Holding the base in one hand, pass the tab through the top slot from the front until it reaches the fold.*

7 *Return the tab through the bottom slit so that it forms a pull handle at the front.*

8 *Pull the tab downwards as you hold the card and the flap will rise like a trapdoor.*

Moving Arm Pop-Up

The moving arm mechanism is constructed by attaching a stick-on arm to the standard 'V' fold. When you open the card the arm moves up to point at the greeting or graphic. By using imagination, you can turn the arm into other graphic shapes.

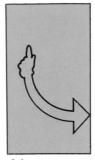

1 *Trace the template of the arm, transfer it to a piece of orange card and cut it out. Take a piece of blue card measuring 20 × 15 cm (8 × 6 in), and fold in half to create a card 15 × 10 cm (6 × 4 in).*

2 *Place the arrowhead on the folded edge of the card, making sure that the hand does not exceed the bottom edge of the card. Trace the arrowhead onto card.*

3 *Using a sharp blade, cut one side of the arrowhead through the two thicknesses of card. Score its counterpart gently with a craft knife.*

4 *Fold back the cut flap along the scoreline. Then turn the card over and fold the flap back the other way to establish a clear fold in both thicknesses.*

5 *Open the card. Pull the top of the cut flap forwards with your finger and close the card to establish the mechanism.*

6 *Align the arrow end of the arm with the left side of the cut flap to check that it fits and that the hand will not stick out from the top of the closed card.*

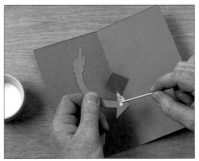

7 *Glue the underside of the arrowhead onto the flap. Hold the arm in place for a few seconds until the glue is dry, then pull the arm forwards and close the card.*

8 *When you open the card the arm should raise and point to the top.*

V-fold

This mechanism is widely used in pop-up books and greetings cards. It consists of a folded shape glued to the card from left to right across the fold. Tabs are used to attach it. When closed, the 'V' shape folds into the central fold of the card and when opened it stands perpendicular to the surface of the card.

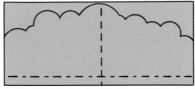

1 Trace the cloud template onto a piece of blue paper and cut out the profile.

2 Make the small incision at the centre of the bottom edge with a knife.

3 Using a stylus and straightedge or ruler, score all the fold lines. Fold the cloud in half along the centre line.

4 Fold the bottom glue tab up and crease it with your finger. Then fold the tab up on the reverse side.

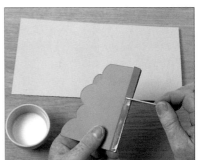

5 Take a piece of yellow card and fold it down the middle. Glue one tab of the cloud.

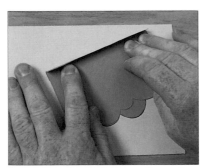

6 Position the cloud diagonally on the card, with glued flap downwards, making sure that the left edge touches the centre fold. Press it firmly for a few seconds until dry. Glue the facing flap into place.

7 Close the card and apply pressure until the glue sets.

8 When you open the card, the cloud will stand up in a V shape; hence the name V-fold.

Skyline Pop-up

Constructing a pop-up scene •

Creating depth using three floating layers •

Creating background and foreground •

ART FORMS

Everyone is fascinated by pop-ups, whether it be a simple greeting card or a magical children's pop-up book. This project employs a mechanism that has been used extensively in both of these applications and is fundamental to the creation of most pop-ups.

The floating layers mechanism permits paper layers to float or project parallel to the base plane. This allows you to create an effective sense of depth using only three layers of paper as demonstrated here. The base plane can be perceived in two ways. If it is vertical, as in this project, the layers float in front of the base. If perceived as horizontal, then the layers float above it (for example, a butterfly on a flower).

The mechanism needs three vertical supports of the same height, attached one at each end, and one at the centre fold. It helps to make roughs using medium-weight paper that can be folded easily by hand. This way, you can experiment with the mechanism and perfect your folds and supports before using your good heavy-weight paper to construct the final pop-up.

When you've completed this project, you may wish to explore the technique further and invent your own variations. It helps to look through pop-up books to identify the floating layers mechanism and see to what ingenious limits you can push it.

A floating-layer pop-up makes a spectacular greetings card. This design would suit a romantic occasion.

SKYLINE POP-UP

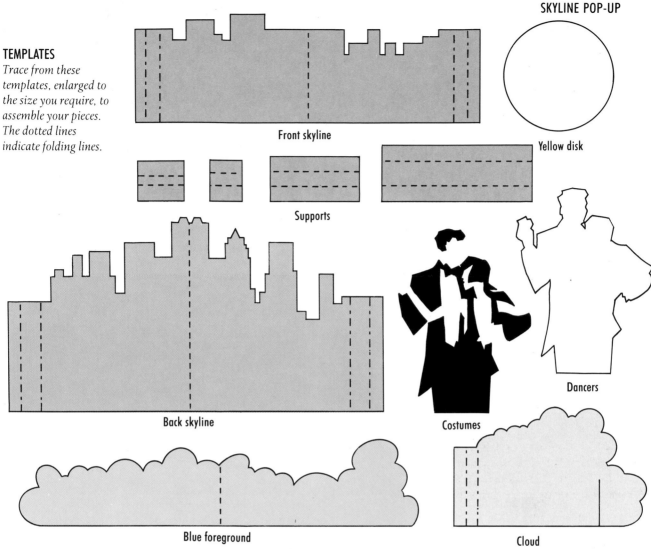

TEMPLATES

Trace from these templates, enlarged to the size you require, to assemble your pieces. The dotted lines indicate folding lines.

Front skyline

Yellow disk

Supports

Back skyline

Costumes

Dancers

Blue foreground

Cloud

CONSTRUCTION DIAGRAM

Here you can see how the separate layers, which appear to float independently of one another, are actually anchored to each other and to the base by supports.

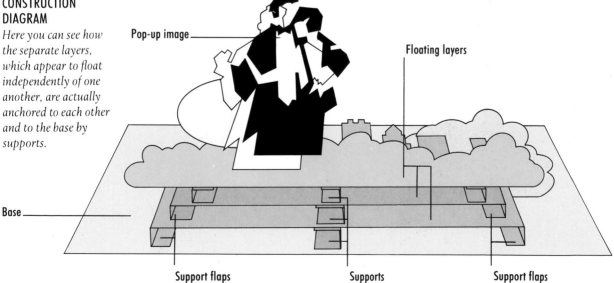

Pop-up image

Floating layers

Base

Support flaps

Supports

Support flaps

1 Begin by tracing all of the templates. Transfer the tracing onto lightweight card in the colours of your choice. Carefully cut out all the shapes using a sharp knife and a metal straightedge.

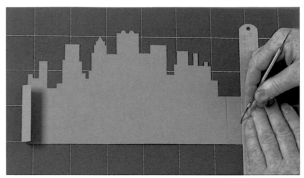

2 With a stylus, score the background skyline along the fold marks. You may need to run the stylus along the pencil line a couple of times to establish a definite scored line. Fold one edge inwards as shown.

3 Repeat this procedure on the other edge to complete the first of the three layers. These tabs will elevate the skyline layer from the card background.

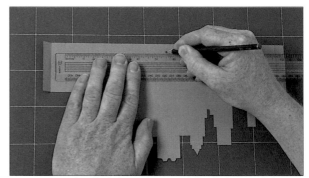

4 Using a ruler, find the mid-point of the skyline, and draw a vertical line down it with a pencil. This will be the point at which this layer folds.

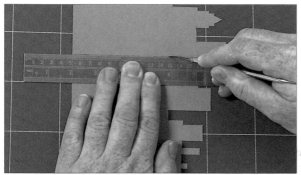

5 Hold a metal straightedge along the pencil line and score the line with a stylus to establish the folding point.

6 Fold the skyline neatly in half along the scored centre line. Run your finger and thumb along the fold a couple of times to establish a good, crisp fold.

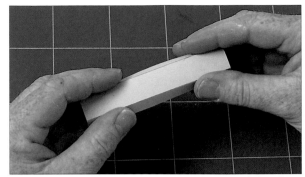

7 *Since this first layer is wide you will need to attach a support behind the centre line to prevent the layer from sagging in the middle. Cut out and score the centre support. This will match the depth of the two end supports.*

8 *Neatly fold the support between your fingers and thumbs along the scored lines to create a three-sided support.*

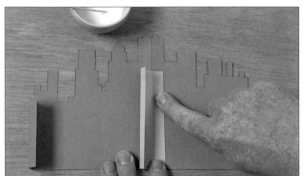

9 *Glue one edge of the support and paste it to the right side of the skyline centre fold as shown. Run your finger along the back of the glued edge to make certain it adheres properly.*

10 *Accurately position the skyline on the inside left of the card, carefully aligning the bottom edges and butting the centre support right up to the centre fold of the card. Accuracy at this stage is critical to the subsequent layers and the operation of the card.*

11 *Lift the support while holding the skyline in place. Carefully glue the card beneath, and press down until glue has set and the position of the central support is established.*

12 *Fold the left tab down and apply glue to it. Close the card to adhere the tab firmly in position. Do the same with the right tab.*

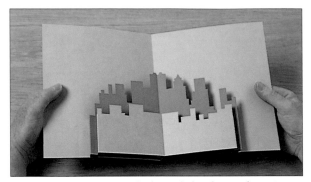

13 *Repeat steps 2–12 on the front skyline layer, gluing it to the background skyline layer. It is important to be accurate when positioning one layer on the other.*

14 *Take the cut-out cloud. Score the straight side along the fold lines with a metal straightedge and stylus. Crease between fingers and thumbs.*

15 *Make the interlocking incision with a knife. This will hold the cloud in place without using glue. As long as one edge is glued to the background, the skyline layer will pull the cloud into position when the card is opened.*

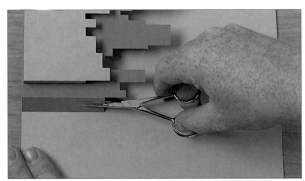

16 *Using small scissors, cut a 2.5 cm (1 in) slit halfway up the background skyline support from the card surface. This will accommodate the slit you made in the cloud.*

17 *Apply glue to the folded support on the side of the cloud. You will need to work quite fast. The cloud must be positioned before the glue sets.*

18 *Carefully slide the cloud into position, interlocking the two slits on the right while holding the support at right angles to the cloud. Close the card and firm down.*

19 Check the mechanism by opening the card. The layers should rise parallel to the base and not lean to one side. The depth of the scene is governed by the height of the supports.

20 Glue one half of the central support to the back of the blue foreground, and the other half to the skyline centre fold. Then attach one end support flap and close the card to adhere it firmly. Repeat with the third support.

21 When you open the card you should have four layers, including the white cloud, that rise smoothly from the background and create a wonderful feeling of depth.

22 Assemble the cutouts for the dancers and paste them to the pink base. Details can be positioned with the point of a knife. If you are using polyvinyl acetate glue you will need to work quickly before it dries.

23 Roll the pieces with a good hard roller so that they stick flat to the base. If you have any edges that are not stuck, add some glue with the point of a toothpick and re-roll.

24 Glue the dancers to the yellow disc and attach the unit to the blue foreground. Make sure that the woman's elbow remains on the left of the centre fold so that the card closes.

Season Change

ART
FORMS

Making an accurate sliding mechanism ●

Dissolving one scene into another ●

Concealing the mechanism ●

Sliding mechanisms make it possible for you to dissolve one scene and create another. This type of mechanism offers great design potential. The intricate sliding construction calls for care and accuracy. You will need to use your protractor to create the angles required for smooth operation. The mechanism consists of two pieces: a base with five parallel angled cuts, and a moving section with parallel angled cuts that interweave with the base cuts. Sliding the moving section back and forth reveals either its picture or the one on the base.

Draw and colour your designs before you cut the parallel strips. If you use photographs mounted on card, glue them firmly, so that they will not catch when you slide the mechanism. The pictures here show a change in season, but could be any two images that suit your fancy.

This project may look complicated at first but provided your measurements are accurate, you should have no difficulty creating a mechanism that transforms one image beautifully into another.

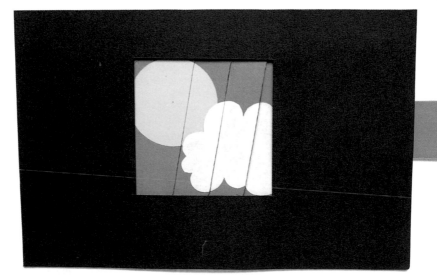

TEMPLATES

Minor variations in the size of the sun and clouds are unimportant, but the two pieces that operate the sliding mechanism must be exactly as shown for the movement to work.

White cloud

Sun

Dark cloud

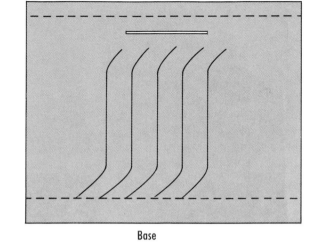

Base

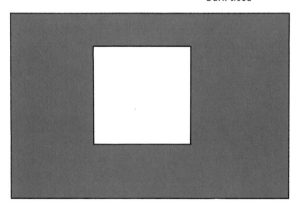

Mask

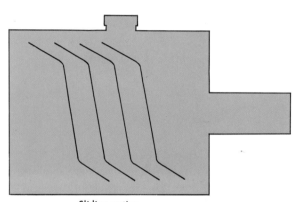

Sliding section

CONSTRUCTION

The mechanism underlying the graphics comprises two pieces of card that slide through each other by means of interlocking slits. These are framed by a mask that provides additional decoration. Add glue only at the corners.

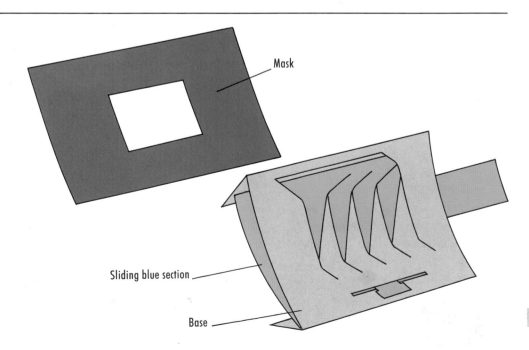

Mask

Sliding blue section

Base

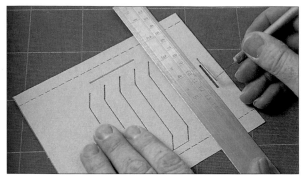

1 *Cut the side and top slits in the pale grey card. Then cut the four central tabs, leaving them attached at the bottom.*

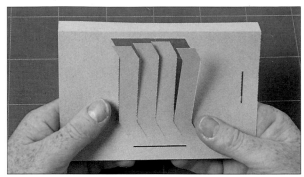

2 *Turn the card over. Score the top and bottom folding lines lightly with a craft knife and fold back. Held up, the card should look like this.*

3 *Cut the three central tabs in the blue sliding piece but leave them attached at top and bottom. Fold the lower tab of the handle up, and the upper part down, to form a triple thickness, and glue into place.*

4 *Cut out the cloud and sun, paste them into position on the blue card and roll them flat.*

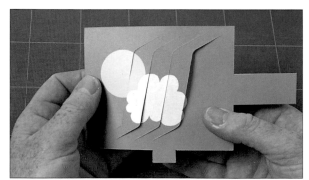

5 *Turn the blue card over and cut the slits again to include the sun and cloud. Check from the right side that you have cut all the way through.*

6 *Glue the dark cloud onto the grey card. Punch out some white paper snowflakes with a leather or paper punch, and add these to the grey card.*

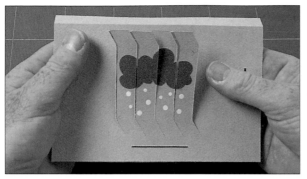

7 *Repeat step 5, cutting the slits through from the back.*

8 *Holding the grey card reverse side up, insert the top tab of the blue card into the slot as shown.*

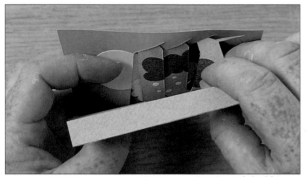

9 *Insert the four grey central tabs into the slots of the blue card, one by one, and then place it flat on the table with the reverse side up.*

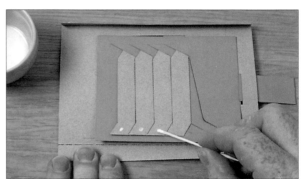

10 *With the blue and grey cards in position as shown, put a dot of glue on the end of each grey central tab and fold the grey edge up to attach. Glue and fold the top edge down so that it does not touch the blue card.*

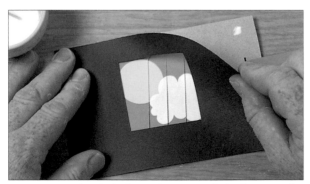

11 *Cut a mask to hide the mechanism, and glue it on top of the grey card at the four corners.*

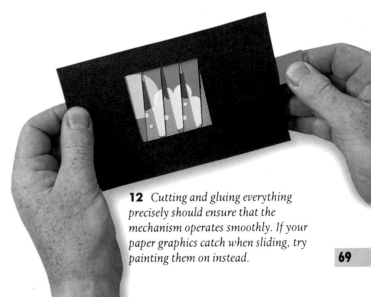

12 *Cutting and gluing everything precisely should ensure that the mechanism operates smoothly. If your paper graphics catch when sliding, try painting them on instead.*

Lion in a Cage

Using a see-through pop-up layer •

Drawing up parallelograms to form layers •

Creating depth using multiple layers •

Hiding the mechanism •

ART
FORMS

This pop-up technique is similar to the multi-slit mechanism (see p. 56). Here, however, you cut out separate planes and attach them parallel to the base planes. It is one of the simplest techniques used in the earliest pop-up books. Provided each layer forms a parallelogram, multiple layers enable you to create images of great depth. Theoretically, you could use any number of layers; in practice you are restricted by the amount of paper that allows comfortable closure of the card.

Make sure your base is wide enough to hide the mechanism when the card is closed or it will spoil the surprise on opening. A multi-layered pop-up is designed to be viewed when the two base planes are at 90°, that is to say, the base would form a floor and a back wall. If you want to view a design from a different angle, turn the base 90° to form a back and a side wall. When you have successfully completed this project, try designing one with twice the number of layers and cutouts.

The cut-out animal makes this simple pop-up mechanism appear more intricate, and a see-through pop-up cage further enhances the effect.

TEMPLATES

The lion templates are actual size and need several pieces of differently coloured card, which are assembled before mounting. The cage is a straightforward three-fold construction from a single sheet of card.

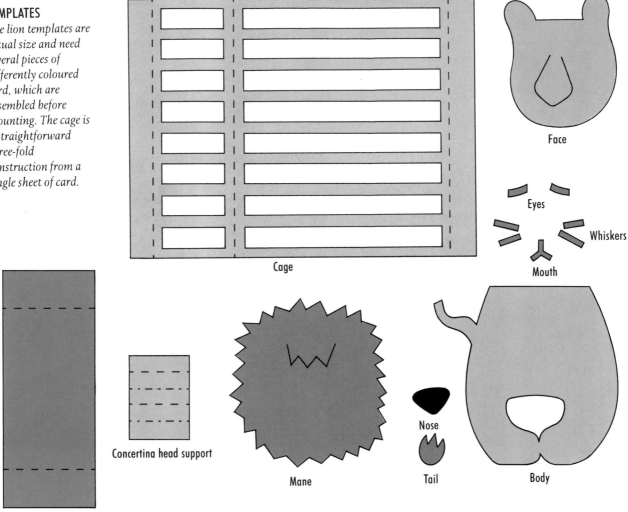

Cage

Face

Eyes

Whiskers

Mouth

Lion support

Concertina head support

Mane

Tail

Nose

Body

CONSTRUCTION

When the card is opened, the cage pops up to reveal a lion whose head is attached to its body by concertina-folded tabs. These keep the head projecting from the body and give the lion added dimension.

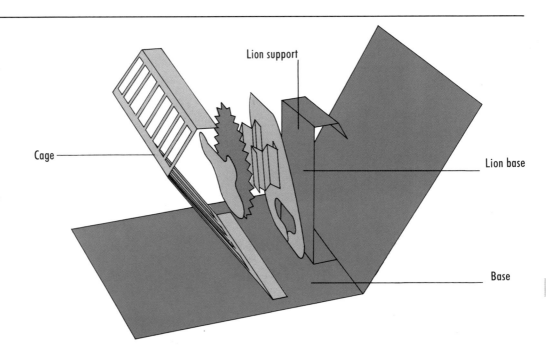

Lion support

Cage

Lion base

Base

71

1 *Trace all the lion templates and transfer them onto thin card: orange for the body and head, and brown for the mane. Cut them out and set aside.*

2 *Trace and transfer onto the same thin card the two concertina head supports. Cut them out, score and fold them. Flatten the folds with a straightedge.*

3 *Assemble the lion's head, gluing the mane, eyes, nose, mouth and whiskers. Spear small features with a craft knife point and apply glue with a toothpick before lowering them carefully into position.*

4 *Paste the plume to the tip of the tail. Then apply glue to one end of each of the concertina head supports and attach them to the body.*

5 *Glue the other two ends of the head supports and fix the head firmly in place.*

6 *Choose a piece of card that contrasts well with the lion and cage, and fold it in half. Cut out, score and fold the lion support, using the same colour as the card itself to make it inconspicuous. The support should be two thirds of the height of the lion's body. Glue one tab of the lion support up to the card fold and hold it in place for a few seconds.*

7 *Fold down the tab at the other end, then apply glue to it. Close the card firmly.*

8 *When you open the card the lion support should pop up. You can now attach the lion to the support. Glue the support first and press the lion to it, making sure that the animal's feet touch the base when the card is open at 90°.*

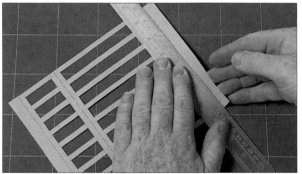

9 *After measuring and drawing the cage on light grey medium-weight card, cut out the bars, score the folds and pull them up against a straightedge to fold them without creasing.*

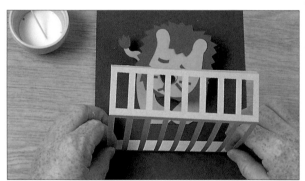

10 *Attach the cage in the same way as the lion support. Remember to glue the cage bottom to the base at the same distance from the fold as the depth of the cage.*

11 *Fold back the cage top and apply a strip of glue along it. While holding the cage down, close the card and keep pressure on it for a few seconds until the glue adheres.*

12 *When the card is opened at right angles, the lion and the cage should be parallel to the back and the base.*

Origami

Origami, from *ori* (to fold) and *kami* or *gami* (paper), is the Japanese art of paper folding. Traditionally the paper may only be folded to the desired shape without cutting, gluing or any form of added decoration. Therefore, origami designs tend to be geometric and do not produce the organic shapes possible with paper sculpture or papier mâché. They do, however, possess the serene simplicity common to many forms of Japanese art.

From our early schooldays we can probably all remember bringing home a folded paper creation formed from a square of coloured paper. Adults also find paper folding a relaxing and fascinating pastime. There is a limited number of basic folds to master, and once you are proficient at these, there is virtually no limit to the designs you can create from a single sheet of paper.

Japanese designs generally use paper that is coloured on one side and white on the other. But any paper that creases well is suitable for origami. Practise on photocopying or writing papers and save your good paper for the finished design.

Precision is the main prerequisite for successful origami. Make sure your paper is perfectly square, and use firm pressure when creasing to flatten the folds. It will usually take a couple of attempts to produce satisfactory results, so don't be disheartened by your first try. You can practise origami almost anywhere, with a minimum of materials and space, and most designs can be flattened and stored for future reference.

TWO-COLOUR IMAGE
The fox is made from a square of paper that is white on one side and brown on the other. It was carefully folded to make maximum use of the paper and the possibilities presented by the two colours. (Fox, Paul Jackson).

CLEVER CREASING
This cheerful locomotive and cars are made of strong wrapping paper, carefully creased into squares. The wheels are created by pleating and tucking (Locomotive, Max Hulme).

CRAFTY CONTAINERS

You can make your own original boxes and bags using origami paper and techniques. Here, the combination of brightly coloured papers and unusual designs results in boxes to treasure rather than discard (Gwynne Radcliffe).

ANIMAL ANTICS

*Animals are favourite origami subjects. The two little mice and the sturdy brown bear show what can be achieved. (*Mice and Bear, *Edwin Corrie).*

TYPES OF PAPER

Try to find paper that is fairly thin but reasonably strong so that it does not tear easily. Most origami designs start from squares, and if you are cutting your own paper it is important that this is done accurately. Toy and craft shops often sell brightly coloured origami paper that has been specially pre-cut into squares (not to be confused with gummed paper squares, which do not fold well), but many types of ordinary paper are also suitable for folding, for example, photocopying paper and plain or patterned gift wrap paper. The important thing is that the paper must be able to accept and hold a crease; softer types of paper (for example, newspaper) will not hold a crease well.

Valley Fold

The valley fold is the basic origami fold. Everything you make will involve this type of crease. For the symbol for a valley fold and other origami symbols, see page 53.

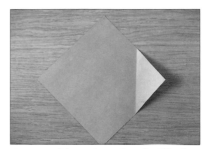

1 With the right side of the paper face up, lift one corner of the paper and form a sharp crease.

2 Viewed from the right side. If both sides are raised, the crease resembles a valley.

Mountain Fold

A mountain fold is the counterpart of the valley fold. Because it is difficult to bend paper underneath itself, it is easier to turn the paper over and form a valley fold. Remember to reverse the paper after you have made the fold.

1 With the wrong side face up, fold over the paper and form a sharp crease.

2 Viewed from the right side, the crease forms a distinctive ridge.

Inside Reverse Fold

The reverse fold is very useful, as it can be adapted to a number of different shapes. This is a triangular shape, formed with a diagonal fold, but you can start with any shape of fold.

1 Fold your sheet of paper in half diagonally. Pull one corner towards you.

2 Form a sharp crease along the corner and then open up the crease.

3 Pinching the centre of the paper with your left hand, grip the right-hand corner and pull down.

4 Tuck the corner inside the main fold and crease firmly.

5 All of the creases that make up the inside reverse fold can be seen here.

Outside Reverse Fold

The difference between an inside reverse and an outside reverse fold is that in an inside fold the part of the paper that moves is reversed inside the paper, and in an outside fold it is reversed outside the paper.

1 *Fold your sheet of paper in half. Press one corner up, away from you.*

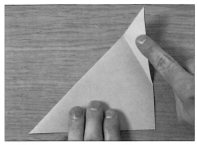

2 *Form the crease firmly and then open out the fold.*

3 *Holding the piece of paper open with your left hand, grip the corner with your right hand.*

4 *Press the corner back so that the wrong side of the paper is revealed, then press the creases firmly.*

5 *When the paper is opened out, you can see that the corner folds have changed from mountain to valley folds.*

Squash Fold

The squash fold involves the simultaneous creation of several creases. Although more demanding than the other basic folds, it occurs frequently in origami, so it is a useful fold to master.

1 *Fold your paper in half diagonally and fold one corner away from you.*

2 *Form the crease firmly and then insert your finger into the fold.*

3 *Using the fingers of your other hand, press the fold back on itself.*

4 *Crease the folds formed by the action in step 3.*

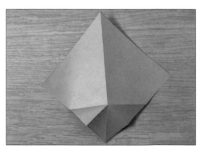

5 *Here you can see the various creases that form the squash fold.*

Windmill Base

The windmill base is an interesting form. It can be adapted by forming only some of the 'sails' into a variety of shapes.

1 *Fold your paper in half horizontally in both directions and then diagonally in both directions.*

2 *Open all folds except the last one. Fold each edge to the centre, opening up after each fold.*

3 *Looking at the back, you can see the complex web of mountain and valley folds that you have formed.*

4 *Turn the paper over. Fold in one corner to the centre.*

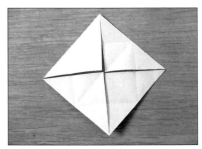

5 *Repeat for all four corners, making sure your folds are clean and accurate.*

6 *Open up the folds and turn the paper over. Press down gently on the four points of the inner square.*

7 *The corners will pop up. Lifting from below, collapse the corners onto the centre square.*

8 *Flatten one corner down on itself, creating a squash fold.*

9 *Repeat for all four corners, so that you have a flat square.*

10 *Turn one of the squash folds outwards, so that the point sticks out beyond the square.*

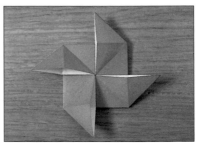

11 *Repeat for the other three squash folds to form the windmill shape.*

Fish Base

The fish base is also known as the kite base. The basic outline shape is very simple, but further folds create a more complex structure that is more adapted for developing other shapes.

1 Fold the paper in half diagonally. Open up. Fold the right-hand corner into the centre.

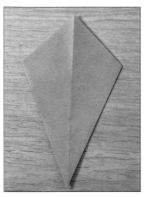

2 Fold the left-hand corner in and turn the paper over.

3 Fold the bottom point up to meet the top point. Press the crease firmly.

4 Turn the paper over towards you.

5 Insert your finger in the top of the left flap and lift, creating a squash fold and a petal fold.

6 Pull out the point and crease in place.

7 Repeat this on the right-hand crease.

Envelope

ART
FORMS

To give your letters a personal touch, you can create your own envelopes using origami. The stylish design shown here is both elegant and practical. The sharp folds and points give the envelope a geometric feel, emphasised by the use of two-coloured paper.

Some of the actions are tricky to achieve because you must manipulate several folds at once, but with practice they are easily mastered. Try them out on some scrap paper before starting on the project. The locking device inside the flap is an interesting feature: it is invisible and yet it holds the point of the flap together and strengthens the whole structure of the envelope.

This project uses three of the basic origami folds – valley fold, mountain fold and squash fold. It is important to practise these folds until you have mastered them as they form the basis for many origami projects.

Manipulating several folds at once •

Incorporating strengthening folds •

Using two-coloured paper •

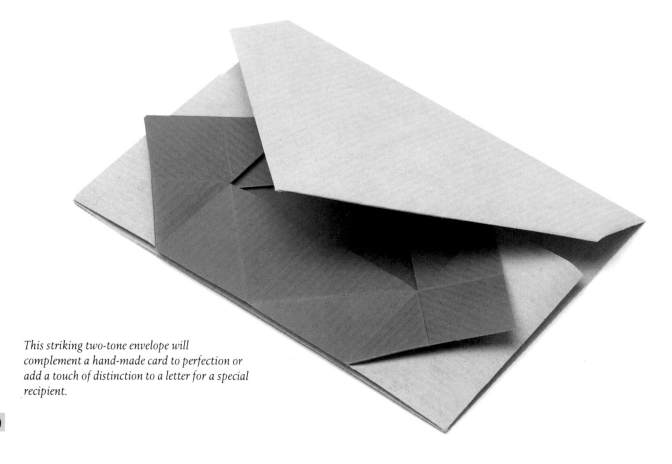

This striking two-tone envelope will complement a hand-made card to perfection or add a touch of distinction to a letter for a special recipient.

1 *Take a piece of paper 38 cm (15 in) square. With the wrong side face up, fold in half. Repeat.*

2 *Make diagonal folds to check that the paper is square.*

3 *Fold in the bottom edge to the centre crease as shown.*

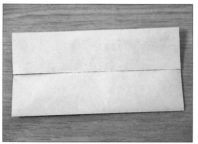

4 *Rotate the paper 180° and repeat on the opposite edge.*

5 *Turn the paper over to reveal the mountain fold.*

6 *Fold the bottom right-hand corner over to the centre crease.*

7 *Repeat step 6 with the top right-hand corner.*

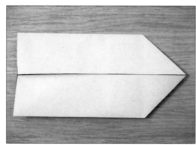

8 *Turn the paper over. The corners are now tucked under to form a point, and the folded edges are revealed.*

9 *Turn the paper so that the point is towards you. Fold over the point, forming the crease to meet the corners of the point.*

10 *Hold either side of the point between your thumb and forefinger.*

11 *Gripping only the outer fold, pull both sides outwards.*

12 *Use your other fingers to tuck in the folds behind the points. This should be carried out in one swift action.*

13 *Press down the crease and make sure that the inner and outer edges of the points align neatly.*

14 *Insert your finger into the right-hand corner.*

15 *Press the squash fold into place.*

16 *Press down the creases. The inner fold has changed from a valley fold to a mountain fold.*

17 *Repeat the squash fold on the left-hand point.*

18 *Insert a thumb under each of the centre corner flaps and lift.*

19 *Grip each corner between a thumb and forefinger.*

20 *Pull each corner outward.*

21 *Change the position of your fingers and press the upper flaps down.*

22 *Press the corners into position.*

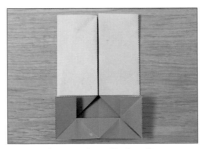

23 *Make sure that all edges line up.*

24 *Lift the left-hand flap.*

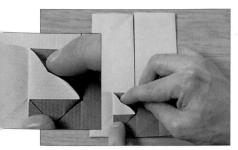

25 Mountain fold the two corners to form a point.

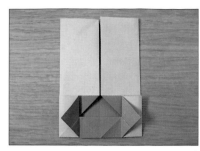

26 Fold the point back firmly.

27 Repeat to make a point on the right-hand flap.

28 To make the flap, fold the top right-hand corner down along the centre line.

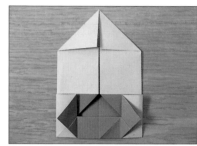

29 Repeat for the left-hand corner.

30 To make the locking device, hold the left-hand corner and grip the tip of the inner fold.

31 Pull the inner point out so that it forms a tab.

32 Press the inner tab inside the flap to flatten and define the creases.

33 Tuck the tab under the right-hand flap as shown.

34 Repeat to make the right-hand tab and tuck that under the left-hand flap.

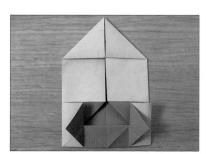

35 The tabs are now invisible, but the flap of the envelope is much stronger.

36 Fold the flap down and tuck it into place.

Gift Boxes and Brooch

ART
FORMS

This project is a variation on a theme that has been popular for centuries, especially in Russia, where peasants used to carve wooden dolls in decreasing sizes that split open and fitted inside each other. Each set could be made up of as many as 12 dolls. This project consists of three nesting boxes, but you could make as many as you wanted.

When presenting the boxes as a gift to someone, what could be nicer than including an extra surprise present in the inner box? Follow the instructions given on page 87 for an attractive brooch. In order to demonstrate clearly the detailed folds, the brooch is made in a larger format. To fit the brooch inside the smallest box, start with a piece of paper 12 x 12 cm (4¾ x 4¾ in). You can purchase a brooch pin from craft shops to stick on the back.

Repeating sequences of folds •

Creating three-dimensional objects •

Using reinforcing folds for strength •

Everyone enjoys the excitement of opening a box and finding another one nesting within it, opening that and finding yet another box, and then finally reaching the treasure at the heart of the stack. Here, a 'jewelled' origami brooch is concealed within three multicolour boxes.

MAKING THE OUTER BOX

1 *Divide your paper into equal thirds by rolling it into place between your fingers as shown.*

2 *Pinch the top of the paper to indicate the position of the thirds.*

3 *Place the paper face down. Using your mark as a guide, fold the left-hand third into the centre and crease.*

4 *Open up and repeat the process for the right-hand third.*

5 *Rotate the paper 90° and again divide the paper into thirds.*

6 *Repeat steps 3 and 4 so that you have four intersecting valley folds.*

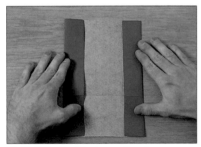

7 *Fold both sides inward, using your existing crease as a guide.*

8 *Open up the folds to reveal the extra crease as shown.*

9 *Fold the top third of the paper down along the existing crease line.*

10 *Insert the fingers of your left hand under the fold, using your right hand to hold it down.*

11 *Make an internal diagonal crease across the central box in the paper.*

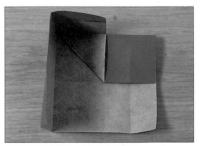

12 *Press the crease firmly into the corner so that the box sides stand up.*

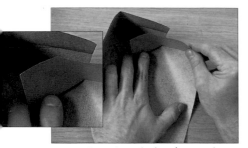

13 Pull up the right-hand corner in the same way.

14 Make a diagonal fold to form a triangle on the base of the box.

15 Make sure that the top edges of the two corners align exactly.

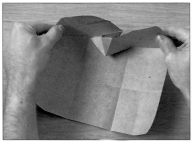

16 Open up the two corners so that your paper is flat once again.

17 Rotate your paper 180° and repeat steps 9–15 to form the last two corners.

18 Refold the corners at the other end along the existing creases.

19 Your box now has four upright sides and a base strengthened by two folded triangles.

20 Lift one of the triangles. Using the tip of the triangle as a guide, fold over the two layers of paper.

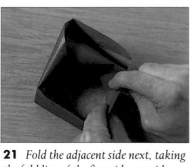

22 Fold down the final two sides and then define all of the corner creases.

21 Fold the adjacent side next, taking the fold line of the first side as guide.

SIZING THE INNER BOXES

Repeat the instructions to make a base and a lid for as many boxes as you require. For each base, your paper should be a 6 mm (¼ in) smaller square than the paper used for the lid. The lid of each box should be a 1.3 cm (½ in) smaller square than the next. These are the sizes used for this project:

Outer box
Lid   25 x 25 cm (10 x 10 in)
Base 24.5 x 24.5 cm
      (9¾ x 9¾ in)
Middle box
Lid   24 x 24 cm (9½ x 9½ in)
Base 23.5 x 23.5 cm
      (9¼ x 9¼ in)
Inner box
Lid   23 x 23 cm (9 x 9 in)
Base 22.2 x 22.2 cm
      (8¾ x 8¾ in)

MAKING THE BROOCH

1 *To start, complete steps 1–9 of the windmill base (see page 82).*

2 *Fold the edge of the top right-hand corner into the centre crease as shown.*

3 *Repeat on the other edge and for the other three corners.*

4 *Holding the points flat in the centre, lift up the flaps to the vertical.*

5 *Squash fold the flap flat.*

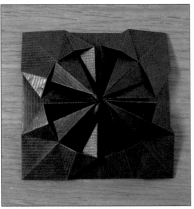

6 *Repeat the squash fold for the other seven flaps.*

7 *Fold back one of the corners, taking your line from the tips of the flaps.*

8 *Repeat for the other three corners, then turn the paper over and define the creases.*

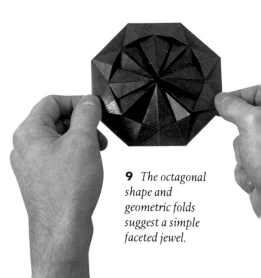

9 *The octagonal shape and geometric folds suggest a simple faceted jewel.*

Origami Camel

ART
FORMS

Using advanced techniques in combination •

Creating and narrowing free points •

Depicting a living creature •

Origami animals are extremely popular, despite being difficult subjects to depict; their curved forms and enclosed volumes do not readily lend themselves to a craft in which straight edges and flat planes predominate. The creative challenge is to find a way to demonstrate their essential form, rather than the detail, so that the creature can instantly be recognized from a few simple shapes. This essential form is achieved first by creating a number of free points to represent the limbs, head, etc. The fish base used here is an excellent starting shape for designing animals, since it has both sharp and blunt free points.

The tricky part of the design comes at steps 25 and 27. The folds themselves are easy, but need positioning accurately so that the head and neck of the camel are properly proportioned. If your first attempt looks a little malformed, unfold back to step 24 and reposition the head and neck creases.

Use a square of thin paper, at least 20 × 20 cm (8 × 8 in). A small dab of glue may be necessary to hold the layers of the hump together. When you have learned to make the camel, try changing the folds to make a giraffe or a llama.

This little group is so atmospheric that you can almost see the sand stretching endlessly beneath the camels' feet. Display them along the top of a bookcase or, to protect them from dust, on a shelf in a glass-fronted cabinet.

1 *First make a fish base using the method described on page 79.*

2 *Separate the two loose corners, pulling them apart.*

3 *Establish a long mountain crease across the middle. The paper remains three-dimensional.*

4 *Gather the layers together. Grip firmly behind the triangles with your left hand.*

5 *Swivel your right hand downwards, flattening the projecting triangles to the right.*

6 *Press the paper firmly flat.*

7 *Narrow the nearside triangle.*

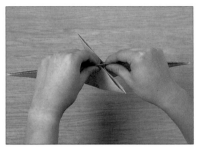

8 *Unfold the crease.*

9 *Narrow the spike at the top left. Note the curved pocket that lifts up. Allow it to stand.*

10 *Unfold. Make a short crease. This connects the intersection of the previous two creases with the bottom corner.*

11 *Form all three creases at the same time by collapsing the paper.*

12 *Press firmly.*

13 Turn the shape over and repeat steps 7–12 on this side of the paper.

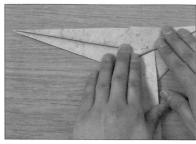

14 Note how the upper corners are now much narrower than in step 6.

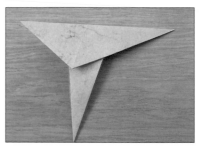

15 Pull the layers apart, allowing the sharp spike to dip and flatten.

16 The spike is now almost flat. Continue to pull the layers apart.

17 Stop pulling when the shape looks like this. Firmly grip the paper at the top and begin to lift the spike.

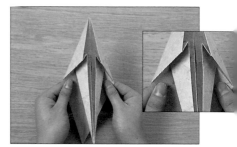

18 Twist the spike out to the right. Flatten and crease.

19 Using the same method, twist the spike out to the left and crease.

20 Squeeze the spike in half, while folding the remainder of the paper in half.

21 Press the paper flat.

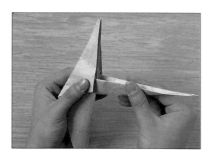

22 Inside reverse fold (see p.76) the lowest corner along existing creases, to its step 23 position.

23 The corner now points to the left. Press the paper flat.

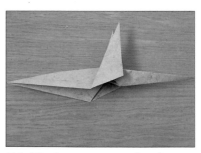

24 Flip the paper over so that the two leg points point downwards.

25 *Valley fold the neck spike.*

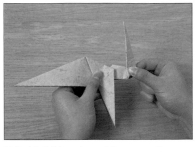

26 *Unfold and outside reverse (see p.77) the spike along the line of the valley fold.*

27 *Similarly, valley fold again to create the head.*

28 *Outside reverse the spike along the line of the valley fold.*

29 *Pull out the layers inside the spike to make a sturdy head.*

30 *Repeat the process on the far side of the spike.*

31 *This is the view of the top of the camel. Fold the tip of the spike inside the head.*

32 *Hold the nose as shown, pulling the layers apart.*

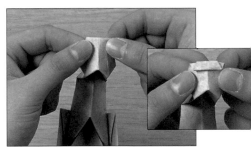

33 *Turn the front edge back on itself to create a thick ridge across the nose.*

34 *The head is now complete. Some of the creases may need repositioning.*

35 *Valley fold the rear leg, as shown.*

36 *Unfold, then outside reverse the leg along the line of the valley fold.*

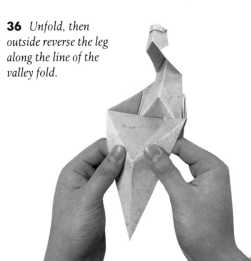

Weaving

Woven paper is an ancient art form that probably originated in Asia. With all of the wonderful papers available today, you can create beautiful designs to frame, or use as greetings cards, bookmarks, table mats, book covers and picture mounts.

Weaving is done by threading the weft (horizontal) strips over and under the warp (vertical) strips. Practise a simple weave of two coloured strips before attempting an irregular pattern of over-and-under permutations using contrasting colours or different textures. Try making hand-made papers from vegetation and recycled paper (see p. 124). Then weave them together in interesting colours and texture combinations to form a geometric design with a beautiful organic quality. Experiment with a variety of weaves, and develop adaptations of your own. Make a three-dimensional weave by creasing some of the warp and weft to create parts that stand out from the rest. Combine this with intricate weaves to create more wonderfully complex designs. Use two identical photographs, or wrapping paper with bold geometric designs, and weave the strips slightly out of alignment to achieve intriguing, double-take effects.

- ✓ Metal ruler
- ✓ Protractor
- ✓ Triangle
- ✓ Craft knife
- ✓ Pencil
- ✓ Glue
- ✓ Scissors
- ✓ Cutting mat
- ✓ Photographs
- ✓ Clippings
- ✓ Adhesive plastic film
- ✓ Papers in different colours and weights

NATURAL PAPERS
The combination of recycled papers, earth colours and a simple woven pattern makes a striking greetings card (Jo Carlill).

BEAUTIFUL BASKETS

Woven paper is very durable and, as seen here, looks like fabric when woven into baskets (Mary Butcher).

WARP

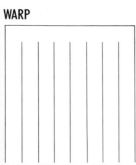

The warp defines the vertical strands of the weave. You can cut them from the same piece of paper, leaving them attached at the top for ease of handling.

WEFT

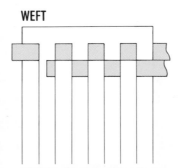

The weft describes the horizontal strands. These are intertwined through the warp. Each weft strand alternates its starting point from the one above.

WASTEPAPER BASKET

Bright paper strips in various widths were woven into this basket. The band at the top was loosely sewn around the rim as a finishing touch (Mary Butcher).

Plain weave

Interweaving paper allows you to create some striking designs. Yet it is one of the simplest of the paper art forms. The 'under and over' plain weave is the best one to start with. The pattern repeats every two rows and appears staggered, much like brickwork. You can create some interesting variations by varying the width of the warp (vertical) and weft (horizontal) strips, or using paper with a deckle edge to soften the hard edges.

1 Take a piece of medium-weight paper 10 × 9.5 cm (4 × 3¾ in) wide. Make four vertical cuts 1.9 cm (¾ in) apart, leaving the top 6 mm (¼ in) intact. Cut five pieces 15 × 1.9 cm (6 × ¾ in) in a different colour for the weft strips.

2 Starting at the top, weave the first weft strip through the warp, over the first, under the second, over the third and so on to the last warp.

3 Take the second weft strip and weave it under the first warp strip, over the second, and so on. Alternate the procedure for the first and second strips for the remaining weft strips.

4 Make sure you push each weft up to the previous one, keeping your weave straight and tight. You can either glue each strip in position as you work, putting a dab of glue at each end, or wait until all the strips are in position.

5 When the strips are firmly glued, trim the edges, and finally the 6 mm (¼ in) top. Glue the remaining strips along the top edge.

Many interesting weaves can be created using the innate qualities of the paper. Choose different textures in a single colour for subtle patterns, or exploit the myriad of coloured papers for eye-catching effects. Utilize old letters, maps, manuscripts, wrapping papers and hand-coloured sheets – experimentation is part of the fun.

Different textures

Three different colours

Irregular weave

Some weaves work best with two colours while others work well with three or four colours. Irregular weaves are mathematical variations of the plain weave and the permutations are endless. Some well-known ones are the zigzag, the patchwork and the shadow blocks weave. The patchwork is an irregular weave that works well using three or four different-coloured papers.

1 Cut your pieces as you did for the plain weave, this time using eight strips 1 cm (³⁄₈ in) wide.

2 Weave the second weft under one warp, over one, under one and so on to the end of the row.

3 Weave the third weft under two warps, then over two warps, and so on. Be sure to keep the strips tight.

4 Weave the fourth weft over one warp, under one, over one and so on to the end of the row.

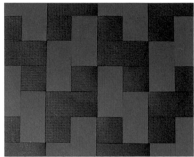

5 Start again at step 1 and repeat this sequence until the weave is complete. Glue and trim as for the plain weave.

Old manuscript

Wrapping paper

Marbled paper

3-D Weave

Unique and unusual wall-hangings can be created by using a 3-D weave. By adding folds to the warp and the weft they project from the surface of the flat weave. If you hang the weaving opposite a natural light source the projections cast interesting shadows that change as the sun moves across the sky.

1 *Cut a piece of yellow paper 23 × 15 cm (9 × 6 in) wide. Make seven vertical cuts to create eight warp strips 1.9 cm (¾ in) wide. Leave 1.3 cm (½ in) intact at the top. Cut eight green weft strips 1.9 × 23 cm (¾ × 9 in) long.*

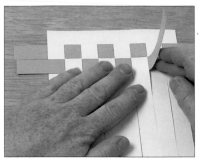

2 *Weave the second strip from the left side, folding it back after the sixth warp strip. Crease the fold with your finger.*

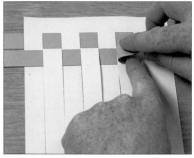

3 *Curl the green strip back on itself, creating a fold that touches the left side of the warp strip. Then fold it back the opposite way, so that you have two valley folds and one mountain fold 1.9 cm (¾ in) apart.*

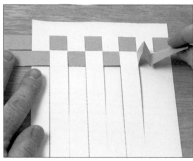

4 *Weave the end of the weft strip over the seventh and under the eighth warp, leaving the folded weft projecting from the surface of the weave.*

5 *Fold the second warp strip upwards and crease. Then fold it back to repeat the complete procedure in step 3, ending with a mountain projection in the warp.*

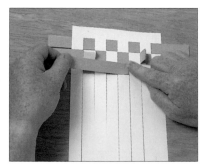

6 *Continue weaving from left to right, as in step 2, but this time folding the strip back after the fifth warp. Repeat step 3. Then fold the third warp strip up and create a mountain projection.*

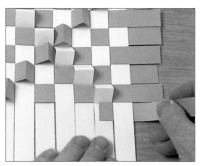

7 *Continue making projections that converge towards the centre, as shown, up to the fourth weft strip. Reverse the entire procedure from the fifth to the eighth wefts.*

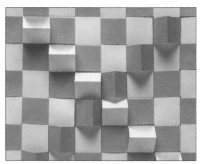

8 *Check that all of the projections are standing up before gluing the loose ends. Trim the woven edges and the top 1.3 cm (½ in).*

Tumbling Blocks Weave

Begin with an orange warp 16.5 × 11.5 cm (6½ × 4½ in) wide. Cut six vertical strips in it 1.9 cm (¾ in) wide. Cut six yellow weft strips 1.9 × 15 cm (¾ × 6 in) long, and weave from the right. **Row 1** *over 1, under 1, over 2, under 1, over 1.* **Row 2** *over 2, under 1, over 2, under 1.* **Row 3** *under 1, over 2, under 1, over 2.* **Row 4, 5** *and* **6** *are repetitions of rows 1, 2 and 3.*

1 *Make eight red strips 1.3 × 15 cm (½ × 6 in) long. Fold one end of each strip to a point so that it will be easier to weave.*

2 *Beginning at the top left corner, weave a red strip over the first warp and under the second weft. Hold the main weave together as you work.*

3 *Turn the weave over and weave the second strip under the third warp from the right to emerge between the second warp and third weft.*

4 *Continue weaving strips from the top to form a gradually evolving pattern of blocks. Proceed to the bottom right corner. Keep turning your work over to pull ends through.*

5 *Glue and trim all of the edges to complete a three-dimensional effect.*

Intricate weaves using narrow strips of paper make beautiful bookmarks. Choose a rainbow of colours, an earthy-toned handmade paper interwoven with the pages of a discarded paperback, or some marbled paper that calls to mind the end papers of an old book. Protect your bookmarks with adhesive plastic film.

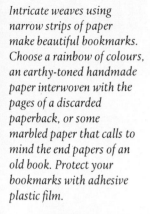

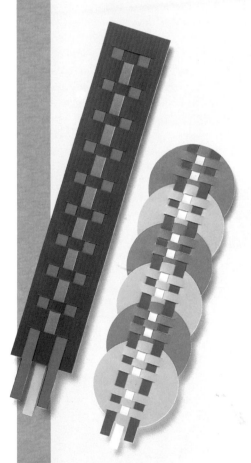

Connect paper shapes by weaving them together with long narrow strips. Or weave a variety of papers through evenly placed slits. Design your own version and include it when giving a book as a present.

Book Cover

Applying imagery and colour to a theme •

Designing a cut-out shape to fit an object •

ART FORMS

A woven book cover can reflect the contents of the volume in more than just design. An atlas cover could combine pictures of sea and land or it could consist of interwoven maps. Weave together seed packets to cover a gardening guide, or old music sheets for a piano book. Make a montage of memorable photographs and hand-made papers to decorate the family album. Wildlife books look striking when covered in enlarged interwoven details of animal coats: zebra, tiger and giraffe skins, or peacock feathers, for example. Again consider the possibility of varying the widths of the strips or incorporating papers with a deckle edge. Use some of the papers that you have marbled, spattered or sponged (see p.46). Covering the weave with adhesive plastic film will keep it clean, however well-thumbed the book.

A treasured book needs protection, and what could be more suitable than a cover of your own design to reflect the contents or enhance your decor? Make a bookmark to match for a perfect gift set.

TEMPLATE

Since books differ in size, we cannot give measurements, but the principle is the same for all. Place the opened book on a sheet of paper. Mark the rectangle formed by the book cover and add the tabs to it as shown.

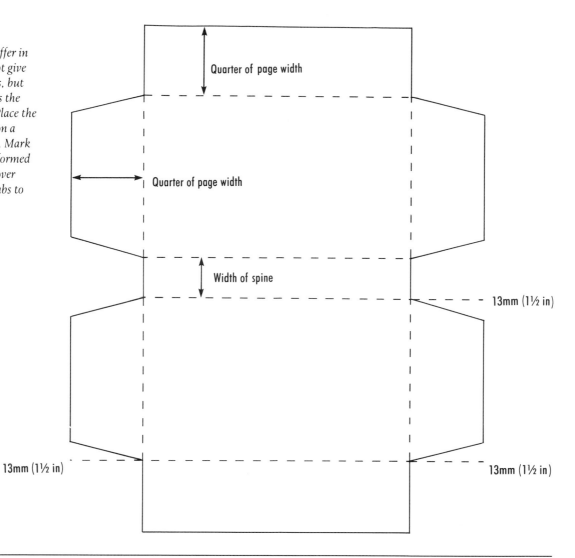

Quarter of page width

Quarter of page width

Width of spine

13mm (1½ in)

13mm (1½ in)

13mm (1½ in)

1 *Return the book to the outlined paper and check that it fits before trimming.*

2 *Cut horizontal slits in the book cover. These will form the weft strips. It is up to you and the size of your book how wide you make the strips.*

3 Turn the corner over and measure and mark the warp strips as shown.

4 Cut out warp strips to correspond. Here, we used 15mm (⁵⁄₈ in) wide strips.

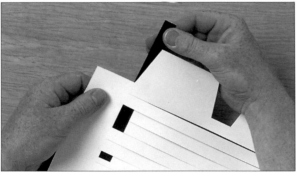

5 Beginning at the top left, weave the warp down through the weft to create a pattern of your choice. Here, a crossword design is being made. Row 1: under 2, over 2, under 2, over 2 and so on until you reach the end.

6 Row 2: over 3, under 1, over 3, under 1, repeat to the end.

7 Row 3: over 1, under 2, over 2, under 2, and so on to the end. Turn the piece over and then butt the strips together to tighten the weave.

8 Row 4: under 1, over 1, under 1, over 1. Repeat the pattern to the end, tightening the weave after each strip is added.

9 *Repeat these four weaving sequences until you reach the right-hand side of your cover.*

10 *It is impossible to butt the strips without leaving a little space, so you might find the last strip difficult to fit. In this case, trim a sliver from it.*

11 *If the strip still sticks, widen the slit by about 1mm (¹/₁₆ in), or just enough to accommodate it.*

12 *Weave the strip through, pulling gently rather than pushing to avoid catching.*

13 *Score the pencil lines along the tabs. Then turn the paper over, fold up as shown and flatten the folds.*

14 *Open the folds and place the book on the cover. Fold up the tabs on the left-hand cover to enclose the book. Repeat on the right-hand cover, and close the book, making sure that the cover fits snugly.*

Greetings Card

Designing greetings cards •

Creating impact with a minimal design •

**ART
FORMS**

Making your own greetings card has a number of advantages. Whatever the occasion, a home-made card carries more meaning than a shop-bought card and can become a unique keepske for the recipient. A hand-made card is always special, indicating that you cared enough to spend time and thought on creating something unique.

In Japan many people make their own cards, decorating them with a sketch, brushwork, wood-block print or stamped image. Paper is a tactile material: the shape, colour and texture of a card made with handmade organic papers appeal to the eye and touch. Use paper made with flowers from your garden, and even perfume them, if you wish, before you weave them. Or copy a letter that your friend has sent you, and combine it with hand-made papers. Vary colour and texture to suit the occasion and the message; the qualities of the materials go a long way in conveying your sentiments. Write your greeting neatly, without flourishes: let your design speak for itself.

*This design illustrates
a two-stage weave:
small strips are woven
through a larger strip,
and that strip is
woven into the card.*

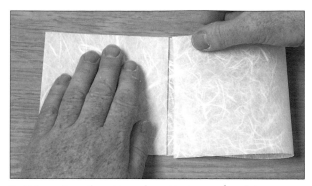

1 *Take a piece of semi-translucent paper, such as Japanese hand-made paper, 12.5 × 51 cm (5 × 20 in) long. Fold it in half, open it and fold each end into the centre.*

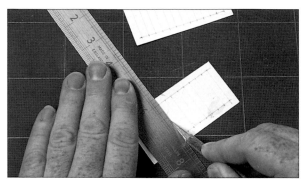

2 *Measure and cut a 4.4 × 9 cm (1¾ × 3½ in) rectangle of paper, and make a series of 13 slits, 3.2 cm (1¼ in) wide, across its width as shown.*

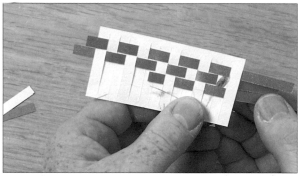

3 *Cut five coloured paper strips 6 × 100 mm (¼ × 4 in) long. Use the five strips to create an irregular weave as shown. Repeat the process with strips of a contrasting colour.*

4 *If you want the depth of the card and the woven strip to be the same, position the strip on the card and trim the excess.*

5 *Make two slits through the four thicknesses of the card in the centre, 4.4 cm (1¾ in) wide and 4.4 cm (1¾ in) apart.*

6 *Slot one woven strip through the front two thicknesses of the card, and the other through the back two thicknesses. The result is a beautifully simple card that relies on the colour and texture of the paper for its design.*

Collage

Collage is the art of juxtaposing photographs, pieces of paper and found objects and gluing them to a surface as elements of a picture. The name comes from the French verb *coller*, to paste.

Découpage is a form of collage. The name comes from the French word for 'cut out'. This art, which was developed at the French court in the 18th century, consists of cutting out printed paper images, gluing them to boxes or furniture, and varnishing them to produce an inlaid effect. To achieve a lacquered effect, you need to apply about 10 to 15 coats of varnish, which makes it quite a time-consuming task.

Although collages were being made as far back as the 12th century, it is generally agreed that the French painter Georges Braque invented collage as we think of it today. Around 1910, both he and Pablo Picasso were experimenting with collage as a new artistic technique. They were soon followed by Henri Matisse who created a series of stunningly simple abstracts from brightly coloured, apparently random paper shapes glued to white backgrounds.

You can use a vast variety of papers in collage, ranging from commercial or hand-made papers to recycled papers such as newspaper clippings, postage stamps and bus tickets. Start to build up a collection, paying attention to colours and textures. The most suitable adhesives for collage are polyvinyl acetate and wallpaper paste, which can be thinned with water.

TOOLS AND MATERIALS

- ✓ 5 cm (2 in) paintbrush
- ✓ 2.5 cm (1 in) paintbrush
- ✓ Polyvinyl acetate glue
- ✓ Wallpaper paste
- ✓ Plastic sheeting
- ✓ Ruler
- ✓ Pencil
- ✓ Scissors
- ✓ Craft knife
- ✓ Papers in a variety of colours
- ✓ Magazine clippings
- ✓ Postcards
- ✓ Music manuscript
- ✓ Wallpapers
- ✓ Gift wrapping and tags
- ✓ Varnish

COLOUR MOSAIC
This colourful composition was created by cutting out each shape and adding it to the work in a particular order, starting with the background and building up to the foreground to create a vivid impact (Flowerscope, *Karen Pathau*).

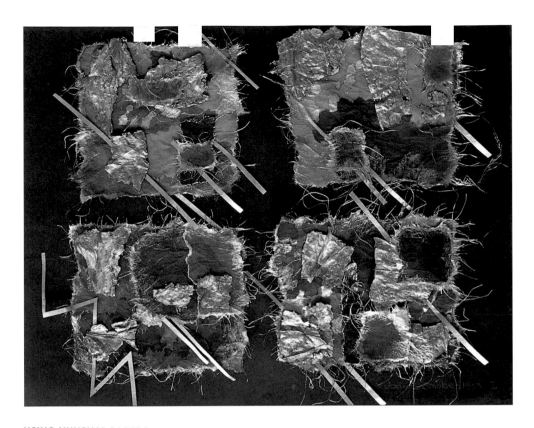

USING UNUSUAL PAPERS
The artist created a textural collage composition using watercolour on pieces of torn Japanese paper. The long fibres in the paper give the torn paper an extra rough edge (One of the 'Golden Series' of paperworks, Joanne Soroka).

MIXED MEDIA
Layers of torn and cut paper have been combined with monoprint, gold paint and white pastel to create a richly textured work. The papers used include recycled chocolate and sweet wrappers. (Sun Worshippers, Mary Chapman).

Overlapping Cut Paper

This technique is very useful for increasing the number of colours you can include in a composition. By overlapping sections of paper, you can combine the colours to create new ones. This technique only works with thin papers such as tissue paper.

1 *Cut strips of paper from different-coloured tissue paper. Choose light and dark shades for maximum effect. Arrange these in place on a piece of watercolour paper.*

2 *Once you are happy with your arrangement, glue the back of each piece of tissue paper and stick it in place. Here you can see the difference between the colours achieved by placing yellow on red, and red on yellow.*

Overlapping Torn Paper

Cut shapes have hard edges. If you want a more muted effect, tear your shapes rather than cutting them. The ragged edge will soften the merging of the two colours and a subtle gradation of tone can be achieved.

1 *Tear out a variety of shapes in tissue paper in a number of different colours. The more ragged the torn edge, the better, so try to tear with and against the grain for variety.*

2 *Lay out your pieces on watercolour paper and try out various arrangements. Here several strips are placed close to one another, creating a rainbow effect.*

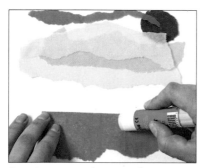

3 *When you are happy with your arrangement, apply glue to the back of each paper shape and stick it in place.*

4 *Flatten out creases with your hand as you go, but remember to handle the tissue paper carefully; it is delicate and will tear or stretch easily.*

5 *The finished composition suggests a sunset over water. The subtle effects created by this technique are useful for natural subjects such as landscapes.*

Crumpling

Sometimes it is useful to be able to introduce texture into a composition. This can be done by crumpling the pieces before applying them to the paper. Combined with gluing of selected areas, crumpling can also be used to create specific structure.

1 *Tear out your pieces and apply some of them flat onto the paper. This composition is of oranges. Select one of the orange shapes and crumple it with your fingers.*

2 *Glue the back of the crumpled orange and press it into place, taking care not to flatten the creases. Add more oranges, combining crumpled and flat ones.*

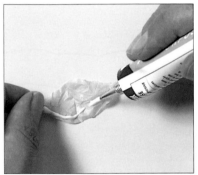

3 *Cut out a leaf shape and crumple it. Using a tube of glue for better control, draw a line in glue on the back to represent the vein.*

4 *Press the leaf into place along the glue line. The creases will lift the leaf away from the paper, enhancing the effect of the vein.*

5 *Add more leaves. As the glue dries, the creases will be pulled in towards the vein line, emphasising the leaf structure.*

GLUING TIPS

When working with paper there are several different adhesives you can use, including polyvinyl acetate (PVA), clear household cement in a tube, glue sticks and glue pens. This chart shows the recommended applications of the main types of adhesive and the art forms they can be used for. Ticks indicate suitability, crosses indicate lack of suitability.

TYPE OF GLUE	PAPER WEIGHTS			ART FORMS
	Heavy	Medium	Light	
Glue sticks	✗	✗	✔	Collage, Origami, Weaving
Glue pens	✗	✗	✔	Collage, Origami, Weaving
Clear glue	✔	✔	✔	Paper Sculpture, Pop-ups
PVA	✔	✔	✗	Paper Sculpture, Papier Mâché, Collage, Pop-ups
Wallpaper paste	✗	✗	✔	Papier Mâché, Collage
Rubber cement	✗	✔	✔	Paper Sculpture, Weaving, Pop-ups, Paper-cuts, Collage
Silicone sealant	✔	✔	✔	Paper Sculpture

Tulips

ART FORMS

This charming picture of tulips is laid on an unusual background. An effect like this is created by weaving strips of tissue paper. The texture is far more interesting than that created by using flat layers of paper. All the elements made from tissue paper were torn rather than cut. This gives a soft effect and contrasts well with the harder, crisper edge of the flowers themselves. These were cut from magazine pages, and appropriate colors were chosen to represent the petals and the leaves.

Fabric paint was used to outline the tulips and also to draw in the shape of the petals. This serves to highlight the main subject of the composition and add detail. Fabric paints are also useful when you need to neaten rough edges.

You can outline the flowers, stem and leaves with dimensional fabric paint. Finally, you can protect this delicate piece by mounting and framing it. A ready-made clip frame is an inexpensive easy option, or you can have it framed professionally.

1 Tear out a rectangle from dark blue tissue paper. It should be 30 cm (12 in) long and 15 cm (6 in) wide. Glue it onto a piece of white watercolour paper.

2 Using a metal rule as a hard edge to tear against, tear off 12 strips approximately 1.3 cm (½ in) wide from a sheet of light blue tissue paper 25 cm (10 in) long. Then tear 16 strips from a sheet 12.5 cm (5 in) long.

3 Place all the long strips side by side. Place the metal rule across the centre of the strips and flip over alternate strips. Place one of the shorter strips parallel with the rule.

4 Lift the metal rule carefully at both ends. Twist it away from you slowly so that the long strips fall back in place. They should overlap the short strip.

5 Repeat this action, butting the next short strip close to the first one. Continue in this way until you reach the end of the long strips, then rotate your work and start to work out from the centre again.

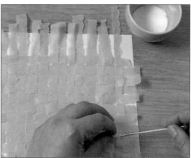

6 Once all the strips have been interwoven, glue the loose ends in place. Use only a drop of glue applied with a small wooden skewer.

7 Allow the glue to dry. Then trim your work by placing the metal rule along the outside strip on each edge and tearing off the loose ends.

8 Divide the woven rectangle in half by carefully tearing all the long strips between two of the short strips. Glue the two pieces in place on top of the dark blue background.

9 Cut out flower shapes from magazine pages. When you are happy with the position, glue the back of each piece and stick it down.

Tropical Reef Lampshade

**ART
FORMS**

Collage is such a versatile art form that it is ideal for cus-tomising objects around your home. The designs can be as focused or as abstract as you wish. Single-subject images are suitable for individual items such as boxes or trays. Or you could link several pieces of furniture, such as wooden chairs, by using the same theme to decorate each one.

For this project we have repeated a motif. The circular structure of a lampshade makes a perfect background for an underwater scene. The fish appear to be swimming round and round. When decorating a lampshade, it is better to choose a paper one rather than a fabric one because it will be more in keeping with the paper applied to it. The one used here is parchment. Whatever type you choose, it is vital to make sure that the shade is fire-retardant.

When the light is switched on, this collaged fish lampshade glows with all the colour and movement of a tropical reef.

MAKING A LAMPSHADE

You can use the same basic method to make a paper lampshade regardless of the size and shape of the frame. Most papers – from newsprint to wallpaper – are suitable, but some will look more effective when the light shines through them.

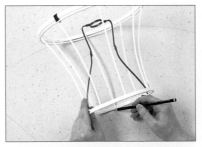

1 *Mark a starting point with pencil on the frame and then roll it across the paper, tracing the top and bottom as shown. Allow a 6 mm (¼ in) overlap.*

2 *Join the lines at each end with a ruler. Cut out. Check the fit. Glue the edges and paperclip until dry. Apply clear glue to the frame rims, insert frame and press into place.*

1 To represent the sea, cut lots of small strips from various shades of blue tissue paper. In order to speed up the process, fold your sheet of paper over and cut through several thicknesses at once.

2 Working on a piece of scrap paper, apply glue to the back of each strip and then stick it in place along the bottom of the shade. Overlap some of the strips.

3 Draw a fish shape on thin card. Cut it out and use it as your template to draw several fish on handmade recycled paper of various colours. Cut these out using scissors.

4 Make a second, smaller template in the same way. Cut out some small fish.

5 Apply glue to the back of each fish along the edge and stick them in place. Position your fish carefully; once you have glued them in place, you will not be able to move them because the glue will tear the parchment.

6 Cut more fish out of crumpled wrapping paper to add further variety. Overlap some of the fish when you position them on the lampshade so that they appear to be swimming alongside each other.

7 To highlight the eyes of the fish, use small, flat-backed glass crystal beads. Glue these into place using a small wooden skewer.

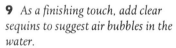

8 Outline the edge of each of the fish with fabric paint. This will hide the glue line, which would otherwise show through when the light is shining through the shade.

9 As a finishing touch, add clear sequins to suggest air bubbles in the water.

Mosaic Box

Mimicking the style of a tile mosaic •
Transferring difficult shapes •

ART
FORMS

This griffin is reminiscent of ancient Peruvian mosaics. The colours have been chosen to reflect this; the earth tones are appropriate ceramic colours.

When you reproduce a mosaic, the first thing you must do is to break your chosen image into separate sections. Each section should represent an individual 'tile'. But do not get carried away – if you have too many small tiles, you will create problems. The image will lose clarity, and tiny pieces of paper are tricky to work with. Practise by tracing images from magazines and other books and breaking the outline into sections. Remember to leave space between some of the sections to allow the background to show through, as grouting would show between real tiles.

You can buy blank boxes in all kinds of shapes and sizes from craft suppliers. Choose a shape that will complement the image you have in mind.

You can confine your decoration to the lid of your box or continue it around the sides as here. Give the whole thing two or three coats of clear varnish when you have finished to seal the paper and protect the box.

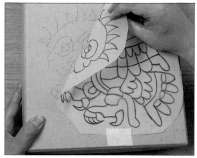

1 *Using a 2B pencil, draw your mosaic griffin on tracing paper. Turn the paper over and draw over all of the pencil lines on the reverse side. Then lay the tracing paper right side up on the lid of your box and draw over the lines.*

2 *Repeat the same process to transfer the sun shapes onto the box. Next, use your traced image to draw the sun pattern onto the back of some gold paper. Cut the individual shapes out using scissors.*

3 *Glue the back of each gold shape and stick it in place on the box. Use the traced pencil image as a guide for positioning the pieces.*

4 *To make the griffin, choose which sections you want to make out of brown paper. Transfer only those sections onto the brown paper using the tracing paper outline. Cut the shapes out using scissors and glue them in place.*

5 *Select sections in turn for each of the other colours or patterns you wish to use. Repeat the same process of transferring the image onto the paper, cutting out the individual shapes, and gluing them to the box.*

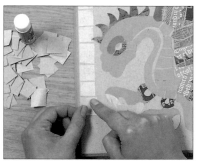

6 *To make the background, start around the outside edge, away from the other images. Cut lots of squares of uniform size, all from the same light-coloured paper. Glue the squares in place, close together.*

7 *As a finishing touch to the griffin, add a tongue. This animates the features and makes the griffin appear even more fearsome.*

8 *Add as many complete squares to the background as you have space for. Where a square would overlap part of the image, trace the outline of the shape onto tracing paper. Use this outline to transfer the shape onto the background.*

9 *Cut out the shape and glue it in place. Repeat this process until the background is complete.*

Paper Cuts

Paper cuts are believed to have originated in ancient China, where they were used to decorate houses, but they are common to many other countries, including Japan, Mexico, Poland, Great Britain and the Netherlands. In the United States, the Amish community in particular are known for their bold folk designs.

Unlike collage or découpage, which normally uses a printed image, paper-cut designs are derived by the artist from sheets of blank coloured paper. Sometimes the paper is folded to give a repeat pattern when cut, such as snowflakes made by schoolchildren. This method is common in traditional designs, notably in Poland where country people adorn their homes with monochromatic cutouts created with spring shears (similar to small sheep shears). Their designs include flower and animal motifs, and often have religious or superstitious connotations.

In the nineteenth century it was fashionable in the western world to display framed silhouette portraits of the family or of famous figures. These were cut out with scissors while the sitter posed. The Victorians loved paper, using it for valentine greetings, educational toys for their children such as cut-out theatres, and Christmas garlands.

Paper cuts can be made with scissors or a knife. Each tool produces different effects. Scissors can vary from Polish shears to fine needlework scissors favoured by silhouette artists. A knife needs a sharp pointed blade for detail and flowing curves.

Paper cutting is used extensively by graphic artists and illustrators, whose work appears in magazines and travel brochures. Don't forget to clip any interesting examples you see and add them to your scrapbook.

TOOLS AND MATERIALS

✔ Pencil
✔ Tracing paper
✔ Craft knife
✔ Masking tape
✔ Stylus
✔ Small scissors
✔ Roller
✔ Cutting mat
✔ Glue
✔ Papers in different colours and weights

LAYERED PAPER-CUT
This is a good example of modern paper-cut art. The artist used a sharp knife to cut out each coloured layer, which he then glued to the background (Red-breasted Goose, David Cooke).

INTRICATE PAPER-CUT

This extremely intricate pattern dates from 1855. The image reflects Swiss rural and town life. Note the contrast between the well at the top and the water pumps at the bottom.

PATTERNED PAPER-CUT

Black makes an effective background for these surreal figures. The decorated papers mirror the title of the piece (Earth, Wind, Water, Fire, Cynthia Gale).

Transferring a Tracing

For many of the projects in this book you need to transfer a tracing onto the paper you intend to cut out. The finished cut-out must face the opposite way from your original drawing, so you can turn it over and it is ready for use. This saves erasing the pencil lines that are then concealed on the reverse.

1 *With a 2B pencil draw or trace your image onto medium- or lightweight tracing paper.*

2 *Place the drawing face down on a sheet of coloured paper and attach the corners with masking tape. Use a hard 2H to 6H pencil to go over the drawing, pressing firmly enough to transfer the image onto the coloured paper.*

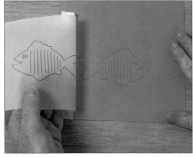

3 *Release the tape at two corners and pull the tracing paper back to check that the picture is complete. If you have missed part of it, replace the tracing paper and go over the drawing again.*

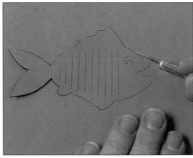

4 *Put the coloured sheet on a cutting mat and cut out your drawing with a craft knife.*

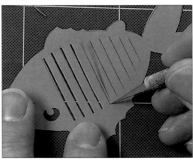

5 *Remove the outline shape from the paper and incise any internal detail.*

FISH MOBILE

Using the fish image (above) you can make an attractive mobile. Begin by cutting out three fish as described, then find their point of balance by inserting a needle through one of the vertical slits in the body and suspending the fish; at the point of balance, prick a small hole in the dorsal fin with the needle. Thread a piece of fine black thread through each fish, then suspend them from a thin wire or light stick and hang them in front of a window.

Cutting and Folding

By selective cutting you can bring some parts of an image forwards and cause others to recede, while keeping the background intact. Shine a light through the completed cutout to give unusual illuminated outlines to the work.

First, transfer your image onto a sheet of paper (see left). Now decide which elements should recede and mark them with a heavier pencil line. These lines will remain uncut.

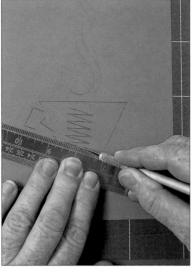

1 *Carefully cut around your image, following the paler pencil lines. The image should remain securely anchored to the paper.*

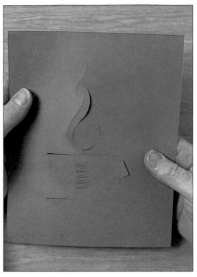

2 *Push the sheet from behind to see where adjustments are needed.*

3 *Ease details forwards and backwards to create slits of varying size that will allow different amounts of light to penetrate the paper.*

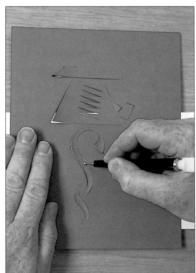

4 *Shape embossed or scored detail with a stylus or burnisher from the underside. Press firmly.*

5 *The result is an embossed piece with some cut edges that conveys an interesting soft and hard effect. Shining light through it creates a glowing white outline with gradated colour.*

Polish Folk Art

Cutting accurately with scissors •

Folding and cutting a repeat pattern •

In Poland paper-cut designs can be found on tapestries, furniture and fabric. This traditional folk art was historically carried out by peasant women. Motifs were usually leaves, birds, geometric shapes and representations of village life, such as harvesting and wedding scenes. Designs, cut from black paper, were usually regional. The Kurpie people, for example, folded their paper twice to produce four identical quarters, and our project is based on their approach.

Although scissors were traditionally used, we suggest a knife for tight corners and details. Use thin paper, which is easy to cut when folded several times, or it will be hard to go into corners without destroying intricate elements. The Poles cut their designs without preliminary drawings, but we advise using a template initially until you gain more confidence. After completing the project, you can devise motifs of your own. An interesting variation, also found in Poland, is multi-coloured: cut the pattern from black paper and apply one or more coloured layers under it.

To make a template, trace a quarter of the design. If you would like to enlarge the design, use a photocopier with an enlargement facility.

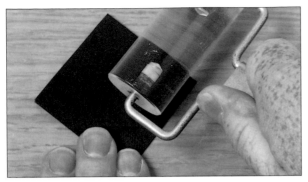

1 Fold a square of black paper in half, then in half again. Use a roller to flatten the folds.

2 Transfer the traced image onto the folded square, making sure that the two joined sides of the tracing correspond to the folded sides of the square.

3 Carefully cut out the pencilled shape, using nail or needlepoint scissors where it is comfortable to do so, and a craft knife for fine detail.

4 A craft knife is essential for internal shapes.

5 The completed pattern should look like this with all cuts going cleanly through all four thicknesses of paper.

6 Open the full-size square with extreme care. There are delicate parts towards the centre that can easily rip. Tidy up any corners that need it and your cutout is complete.

Art Deco Box

Working with coloured layer cutouts •
Decorating a 3-D object •

ART FORMS

This project applies the principles of traditional Chinese paper cutting (see p.9) to Art Deco – the Cubist-derived style of the 1920s and 1930s that embraced fine and industrial art. The main image is cut from black paper, colour details are applied to the reverse in separate pieces, a sheet in another colour is stuck to the back and the assemblage is mounted onto a cardboard box. The resulting object resembles boxes of the Art Deco period that were constructed of wood veneers or of silver with an embossed image. It would make an ideal gift in its own right, or could be filled with sweets.

Use the same technique to mount the design onto an existing wooden box, and seal it with several coats of varnish in a similar way to de-

coupage (see p.104). Or attach transparent coloured paper behind the black paper cutout and hang the finished piece in front of a window like a stained glass plaque so the light can shine through. When selecting an image you will need to consider the shape and size of the object to be decorated. If you find an image which is the right shape but the wrong size, you can enlarge or reduce it on a photocopier with an enlargement facility.

The simple shape and contrasts of this technique are ideally suited to an art deco effect. However, you could achieve very different effects depending on your choice of colour and image.

TEMPLATES

Make an enlarged photocopy of these templates to the size you require. Be sure to transfer the colour mark-up to your set.

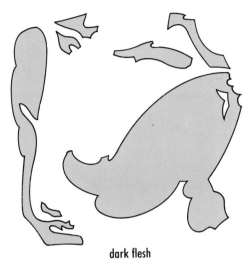

dark flesh

light flesh

This technique works well with an image that has strong contrasts. If the image you have chosen has too many subtleties, you can easily simplify it. This paper-cut was taken from a photo of an Art Deco stone relief. By placing tracing paper over a photograph you can trace the shadows, thus reducing the image to black and white. Here, colour was added to represent flesh tones. Create your own subjects on camera by silhouetting them against the light, or trace high-contrast pictures from magazines.

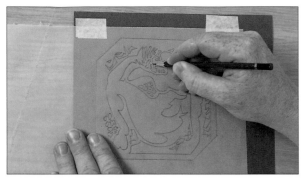

1 *Trace the black template and transfer it to a piece of thin black paper that is easy to cut.*

2 *Cut out the image, cleanly defining each corner and taking care not to sever any connecting pieces.*

3 *Trace and cut out the dark flesh pieces. Paste them evenly to the back of the black cutout, using dots of glue applied with a toothpick.*

4 *Glue the back of the assembled cut-out to a sheet of light flesh-coloured paper, and press it down firmly with a plastic or rubber roller.*

5 *Turn the piece over to make sure no glue has oozed from the side. Then paste and attach the final dark flesh piece. Check that all parts are securely glued to the light pink sheet.*

6 *Roll the assembled cutout again with a plastic or rubber roller. If any parts are insufficiently attached, lift them slightly, slide a glued toothpick underneath, and push them into place.*

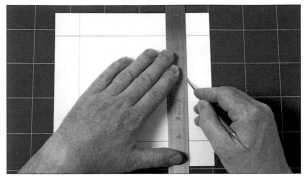

7 To make the box, take a 23 cm (9 in) square of pale blue card (ours is blue on one side and white on the reverse). Draw a line parallel to and 3.8 cm (1½ in) from each edge of the underside. Score the lines.

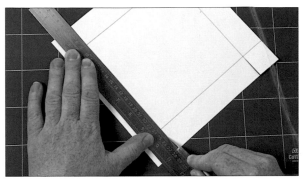

8 Make two 3.8 cm (1½ in) cuts from the top edge along the pencilled line. Repeat on the bottom edge. These will be your glue tabs when you assemble the box lid.

9 Fold all four edges forwards to make a box, bringing the blue, or outer, side over the white, or inner, side. Crease the scored lines with your finger, and roll all of the folds.

10 Open the folded lid and place it top side up. Glue the assembled cutout thoroughly on its underside, turn it over, and position it on the blue lid. Centre it to leave an even strip of blue all around, and press in place with a roller.

11 Bond the lid by applying double-sided tape to the four corner tabs. Peel away the backing strip and turn the lid over.

12 Fold up the edges and tuck in the corner tabs, pressing them against their neighbouring edges to create neat corners. Make another box of the same depth (3.8 cm/1½ in) but 3 mm (⅛ in) shorter to form the base. Fit the lid to the base.

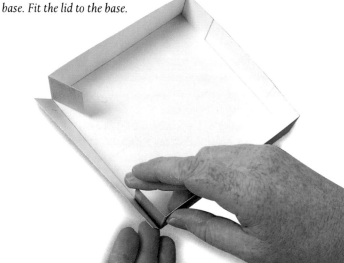

Papermaking

ART
FORMS

Paper plays an enormous part in our lives. We use it to record our ideas, package our products and store the world's knowledge. We turn it into wall coverings and screens, lampshades, boxes and clothes. Yet little thought is given to paper as an art form.

Paper is simple to make and needs little equipment: fibre (from plants, rags or existing paper); water; a liquidiser or heavy implement for beating the fibre into pulp; a large bowl; pieces of felt or other absorbent material; and two boards. The only special item you need is a mould and deckle — a pair of wooden frames, one of which (the mould) is covered with a mesh screen. The mould and deckle scoops up the pulp and allows it to drain while the sheet is forming. The sheet is then turned out onto a felt-covered board, or couched, before being pressed and dried. You can buy a mould and deckle from a craft supplier, but it is easy to construct your own (see p.126).

Paper consists mainly of cellulose fibre, which is present in all living plants. The most suitable plants for papermaking are those with long cellulose fibres that bind to form strong sheets. Hemp and flax are among the best. Cotton rags also make fine paper, because they contain the long, durable fibres of the cotton plant. However, the raw fibres from plants and the processed fibers from cotton rags must first be broken down by prolonged soaking and 'cooking' in an alkali solution. A more practical source of papermaking fibre is 'half-stuff': partially processed fibres and cloth waste from the textile industry, which can be obtained from papermaking suppliers. Existing papers can also be easily recycled.

Colour your paper by making it with coloured material, or adding water-soluble dyes to the pulp with an appropriate binder. Incorporate flowers, feathers and coloured threads. Your reward will be a unique paper hand-made by a process that is over 2000 years old.

TOOLS AND MATERIALS

- ✓ Mould and deckle
- ✓ Vat or plastic tub or deep cat litter tray
- ✓ Liquidiser
- ✓ Felt
- ✓ Pressing boards
- ✓ Sieve
- ✓ Plastic buckets and bowls
- ✓ Scissors
- ✓ Large soft brush
- ✓ Waterproof sealant
- ✓ Polystyrene sheet
- ✓ Waterproof tape
- ✓ Spatula or knife
- ✓ Soft brass wire
- ✓ Small pliers
- ✓ Needle and thread
- ✓ Fine wire shape
- ✓ Half-stuff, assorted recycled papers, plant fibres

COMBINED MEDIA
*The artist skilfully combined coloured and layered paper (recycled from an old bible) with machine stitching to create an unusual paper quilt (*Down to Sleep, Cas Holmes*).*

INCORPORATED NATURAL MATERIALS
This sculptural work combines moulded paper with the main constituent that was used to make the paper, namely wood (Paper and Twigs Sculpture, S. Benechis).

LAYERED AND EMBEDDED
This organic and delicate-looking bowl was made by layering paper over a mould and embedding leaves in the layers of paper to achieve a translucent effect (Large Vessel with Leaves, Maureen Hamilton-Hill).

COLOURED PULP
This colourful piece consists of layered papers that were coloured before being pasted onto the blue background (Dreamer's Stretch, Akiko Sugiyama).

Making a mould and deckle

The mould and deckle is the essential tool for papermaking, because it is the device on which the pulp of fibre and water begins to form a sheet of paper. Although referred to and used as a single tool, it consists of two separate wooden frames. These are identical except that the mould is covered with mesh. The pulp drains through the mesh while held in place by the deckle, which defines the shape of the sheet.

1 Take two strips of wood 30 cm (12 in) long and two strips 20 cm (8 in) long × 1.3–1.9 cm (½–¾ in) thick. Pencil a mark 1.25 cm (½ in) from the end of each strip on either side. Cut a groove to half the depth of the strip, and chisel out the waste.

2 Assemble the frame, interlocking the chiselled grooves. Glue the joints together with waterproof wood glue. Press them firmly into place, and allow to dry completely.

3 To reinforce the joints, drill a hole and insert a 1.3 cm (½ in) screw in each corner.

4 Seal the screw holes and any gaps in the joints with wood filler, using a craft spatula.

5 Rub the frame with fine sandpaper to remove any roughness, paying special attention to the joints. Then paint it with waterproof varnish to protect it while immersed in the vat.

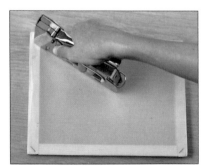

6 Cut a piece of wire mesh to fit the frame and attach it with a staple gun, using stainless steel staples. Staple the corners first so that the screen is evenly stretched.

7 Apply waterproof adhesive tape to seal the edges of the screen and cover the staples. Trim the corners neatly.

8 Repeat steps 1 to 5 to make your deckle. It fits exactly over the mould, ready for use.

Making pulp

The basis of paper is pulp: a semi-liquid mixture of beaten cellulose fibre. Beating causes the fibres to absorb water and unravel. This promotes the bonding that will turn the fibres into paper. Half-stuff, along with other semi-processed textile fibres, and existing papers, are easy to pulp in your kitchen. Soak them in water overnight (or for at least two hours) to loosen the fibres and remove unwanted material.

1 Cut a 10–15 cm (4–6 in) square of half-stuff into strips 3.8 cm (1½ in) wide and then into 3.8 cm (1½ in) squares. Soak in clean water.

2 Place the squares in an electric blender three-quarters full of warm water. Blend thoroughly in two short bursts of 10–15 seconds to obtain a liquidised mixture with evenly distributed fibres.

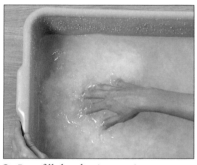

3 Part-fill the plastic container, or vat, with warm water. You will need about 4 blender goblets of water for each blender of pulp, but be sure to leave a gap of at least 7.5 cm (3 in) at the top of the vat. Pour in the pulp and blend evenly.

4 Recycle scraps of paper to lend colour and interest to your pulp. We used postage stamps. Whatever your chosen paper, tear it into small pieces, soak and liquidise it as you did the half-stuff.

5 Add the recycled pulp to the pulp in the vat and agitate once more to mix. The random effect of the coloured paper will be very attractive when the pulp is formed into a sheet.

COLOURING PULP

Recycled paper is only one means of colouring your pulp. You can use natural dyes – from berries, barks, indigo and other plant juices – food colouring, water-based paints and inks, textile dyes or pigments specially designed for colouring pulp. Pigments are available, dry or dispersed in water, from papermaking suppliers and give rich colours. They come with a binder, known as a retention agent, which bonds them to the fibres.

Pigments give clear, vibrant colours. Store pulp in a plastic container covered with a cloth in a cool room.

Forming paper

Forming a sheet of paper calls for a swift, steady hand, but a little practice is all you need to get the hang of it. Try to scoop, lift and shake the pulp in one smooth action. Before beginning a sheet, stir the pulp gently with your hand to ensure even distribution of the fibres. Left to themselves for more than a few minutes, they constantly gravitate towards the bottom of the container.

1 *First wet your mould. Immerse it in water or hold it under running water until it is thoroughly soaked.*

2 *Place the deckle on top of the mould. Hold the mould and deckle together, with the screen in the middle of the 'sandwich' making sure that they are perfectly aligned.*

3 *Scoop the mould and deckle deeply into the pulp on the far edge of the bowl, and pull it towards you.*

4 *In one fluid motion, lift the mould and deckle cleanly away from the pulp. Keep it horizontal so that the pulp held within the frame does not tilt.*

5 *As soon as the mould and deckle is clear of the pulp, gently shake it from back to front and from left to right to help the pulp settle uniformly on the mesh. Stop as soon as the water has drained through the mesh.*

6 *Rest the frame on the side of the bowl while any excess water drains away. Alternatively drain it on a wad of newspaper.*

7 *Very carefully remove the deckle, making sure that you do not disturb the edges of the sheet. Avoid dripping water from the deckle onto the pulp, which could cause 'holes' in the paper.*

8 *You can now see your sheet clearly formed with the characteristic, wavy, deckle edge of handmade paper. It is ready for immediate couching.*

Use silver or soft brass wire (.030–.040 gauge) from a jewellery supplier, florist's wire or any rustproof alternative. Bend this into the desired shape, and stitch it onto the top side of the screen on your mould. Snip off the loose ends of thread on the underside of the screen so that they will not affect the outline. When the wire is in place, form and couch your sheet.

Personalise your paper by creating individualised watermarks.

Couching

Once you have formed a sheet of wet pulp on the mould you will need to transfer it to a flat surface so that you can continue to use your mould and deckle to make additional sheets. This is known as couching. Before forming your sheet, prepare a couching board and a piece of felt or other absorbent material – a square of old blanket, a thick old towel, or an all-purpose kitchen cleaning cloth – to receive it.

1 *Use a firm, varnished board 10 cm (4 in) wider than your sheet on all sides. Drill a hole at each corner to receive the bolts you will need later to press the paper (see p.130). Position damp felt over the board.*

2 *Rest one of the long edges of your mould along the board as shown.*

3 *Swiftly flip the mould over so that the pulp sheet is face down on the felt. Press down on the sides of the mould.*

4 *Lift off the mould by raising the edge nearest to you and using a firm rolling action toward the opposite edge. This helps the sheet to adhere evenly.*

5 *The mould should come away cleanly, with little or no traces of pulp sticking to it. Place another piece of felt on top of the couched sheet and repeat the same process for other wet sheets.*

Pressing

Once you have couched and layered the number of sheets you need, you must press them. This does two things: it squeezes out the excess water before drying and it helps to bond the fibres, so strengthening the sheet. Make your own press by adding a second wooden board to the pile of paper and felt and screwing it to the base board.

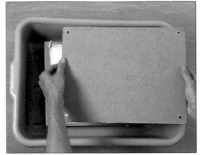

1 Place a varnished wooden board, identical to the base board, over the top felt sheet and screw it to your base board using 7.5 cm (3 in) bolts and wing nuts. Raise the press on two pieces of wood and leave it in a container.

2 After about 30 minutes, take the press from the container and remove the top board and felt. Carefully lift the next felt, with the sheet of paper on it, by diagonally opposite corners.

Drying

You can leave your sheet on the felt to dry, but this can be a slow process. Drying is quicker if you transfer the sheet to a smooth surface by upturning and removing the felt. If you find it difficult to turn your sheet out, place a piece of acetate over the top and turn over all three layers.

1 Place your sheet with the felt uppermost on a flat, clean, waterproof surface. Use a wide, soft brush to brush from the centre to the outer edges of the felt. This will help the paper to adhere to the surface.

2 Carefully peel off the felt. Brush the paper to remove any loose surface fibres, and leave to dry overnight.

CREATING A RELIEF IMAGE

As an alternative to embossing a finished piece of paper (see p.40), you can create a relief image within the sheet as you are pressing it. One simple method is to use a waterproof stencil. Place it on the couched sheet and cover it with a piece of felt (or other absorbent material). To make sure that the stencil is pressed firmly into the pulp you will need to add several more layers of felt before you press and dry.

Subtle effects can be achieved with a relief image.

Embedding

There is endless scope for incorporating objects within a sheet of paper as you form it. Natural objects are especially suitable, but you can also create interesting effects with manufactured items, such as sweet wrappers. The only criterion is that they be flat.

1 *Arrange the leaves on the mould. Once you have decided on their position, remove the leaves and mask the areas on which they will sit with masking tape.*

2 *Form and couch the paper. The pulp will only settle on the unmasked areas, forming four separate strips.*

3 *Place the leaves on the couched 'sheet' in the positions you had chosen. Press the tips that overlap the pulp firmly to anchor them.*

4 *Remove the masking tape from the mould and form a second, entire, sheet of paper. Couch this directly on top of the original sheet, aligning the edges as closely as possible.*

5 *Allow the paper to dry. The second sheet will seal the leaves in place, but they will show clearly leaf side upward.*

Casting

You do not have to restrict yourself to making flat sheets of paper. You can make three-dimensional shapes using everyday objects such as this sieve as moulds.

1 *Work with sheets that have been only lightly couched and so are still damp. Remove a triangular piece from the corner of a sheet by tearing against the blade of a blunt knife.*

2 *Lay the triangle into the mould. Add more triangles, overlapping the edges to create a seamless effect. Build up several layers in the same way, and leave to dry. Gently ease the cast from the sieve.*

Aromatic Paper

ART FORMS

Hand-made scented paper is both attractive to look at and delightful to smell. These sheets are ideal for using as notepaper for a special letter, or even for folding into envelopes. Sprinkle scented ingredients into your pulp for a textured, lightly perfumed effect, or blend scent into your pulp for a stronger fragrance. Your choice of scented ingredients is limitless, but be careful when using artificially dyed products, because they tend to bleed. Test for this by wetting the material. If the colour runs, the dye is not fast and it will leak into your paper. This is less important if you are pulping your ingredients, and indeed you may want to create the effect deliberately.

Incorporating natural objects •

Creating scented paper •

Combining colour, texture and scent •

These delicate, scented sheets will be treasured by the recipient of a letter written on them.

SCENTED PAPER

1 Select the dry ingredients that you want to include. If you are using flowers on stems, such as lavender, shake the flowerheads off and discard the stems.

2 After making a batch of pulp and colouring it (see pp.126–7) to match your scented ingredients, mix the pulp with water in the vat.

3 Sprinkle the lavender flowers evenly into the pulp.

4 Agitate the pulp with your hand to ensure that the flowers are mixed well.

5 Form, drain and couch your sheet of paper. The texture will add visual interest to the delicate smell.

POT POURRI PAPER

1 To make a more strongly perfumed sheet, use scented pulp. Liquefy a pot pourri of scented wood shavings in an electric blender three-quarters full of water.

2 Add the scented mixture to some coloured pulp in the vat and mix well.

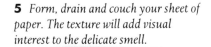

3 Form the sheet. The sheet will have a more regular surface than the lavender paper. Couch your sheet on top of the first lavender sheet.

Shaping Paper

Creating unusual shapes •

Masking areas on the mould •

Embedding objects within layers •

ART FORMS

Once you have mastered the basics of forming and couching, you can adapt those techniques to create more unusual pieces. Make your own irregularly shaped deckles, or utilise other craft frames, as we have done here. Masking areas on the mould gives further flexibility of shape.

Simple deckle shapes can be cut from plywood with a jigsaw. You can also use biscuit cutters, cake moulds, or a product called Buttercut (available from papermaking suppliers). If you are making stationery papers an envelope-shaped deckle is convenient. Experiment with hearts, stars, animal shapes and festive figures such as angels.

Here, three separate couched sheets were layered. There are two benefits to this technique: the varying thicknesses of the pulp over different areas gives a pleasing effect; and if you want to use heavy items as embellishments, they can be anchored between the layers.

To preserve this fragile creation from dust and damage, it will need to be placed in a deep frame with a glass front.

1 To make a basic circular mould and deckle, stretch a piece of nylon curtain over a 30 cm (12 in) diameter embroidery frame. Tighten the outer ring and then trim off any excess nylon to the edge of the hoop.

2 Using a template, draw two semicircles on waterproof tape. Cut these out. Use the same template and a soft pencil to draw a circle on the centre of the screen. Stick the tape in place using the pencil mark as a guide.

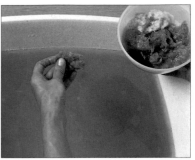

3 Use two or three different pulps. This will give an unusual effect to the finished piece. Add all the pulp to the vat and agitate well. A combination of half-stuff and pulp made from natural fibres was used here.

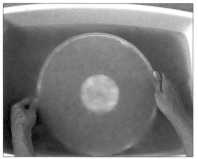

4 Form your sheet. You will notice that pulp will not adhere to the masked area, and so a hole will appear in the centre of the sheet.

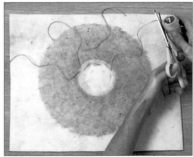

5 Couch the sheet. While it is still wet, apply lengths of string from the middle ring to the outside edge and beyond. As it becomes wet, the natural colour of the string will be absorbed into the paper and leave a 'printed' line.

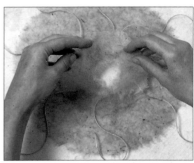

6 Make a small circular sheet in the same way as the first one, using a 14 cm (5½ in) embroidery hoop mould. Mask the centre. Laminate this sheet on top of the first one, trapping the string. Brush out with a soft brush.

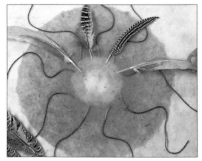

7 Add feathers to the wheel, positioning them in such a way as to make a pleasing design with the string.

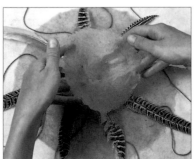

8 Form another circle of paper using the smaller mould, but do not mask the centre. Place this solid circle over the centre of the wheel, covering the base of the feathers. Take care when handling, as the circular sheet is fragile.

9 Use the soft brush to secure the feathers, and sponge off any excess water. You can now add decoration, such as knotting the ends of some of the strings or attaching tiny shells.

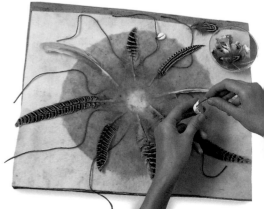

Cast Paper

Creating deep relief •

Constructing a mould •

Casting from a shape •

This cast paper piece was constructed using a simple shape. The geometric pattern is effective, but almost any shape can be made. The only guideline is that it should have sufficient depth to create a three-dimensional relief. If your cast shape is too shallow the effect will not be very different from that created by embossing a thick sheet. The deeper the relief, the greater the contrast between the two sides. Display whichever you prefer, or make two pieces from the same mould and present them as a pair, showing alternate sides.

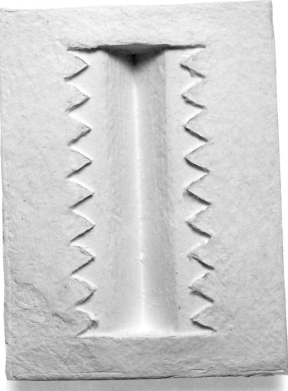

The two sides of a mould look very different. Display whichever you prefer or make two pieces, perhaps using a contrasting colour, from the same mould and display different sides.

1 *Construct a box 3.8 cm (1½ in) deep, using four strips of waterproof, varnished wood and a wooden or plastic-coated board for the base. The strips should be 1.3 cm (½ in) thick × 5 cm (2 in) deep and the board 1.3 cm (½ in) thick. The ends of the strips can overlap.*

2 *Screw the strips together with 1.9 cm (¾ in) screws. The strips should fit tightly around the base board but need not be screwed to it.*

3 *Seal all of the inner joints with silicone bathtub sealant, then turn the box over and seal the joints on the bottom. Leave to dry.*

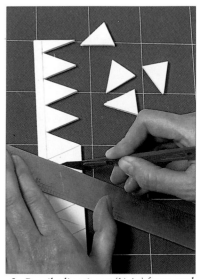

4 *To make the cast, draw four long strips and two small triangles on card. Cut out the shapes and glue two of the strips together along their long edge, using waterproof adhesive tape. Angle the glued edge to form a raised 'tunnel'.*

5 *Glue the end triangles in place, and set aside to dry.*

6 *Pencil a line 6 mm (¼ in) from, and parallel to, the long edge of the third strip. Draw a row of triangles with this line as their base and cut them out, using a sharp blade against a straightedge, to form a serrated pattern. Repeat this method for the fourth strip.*

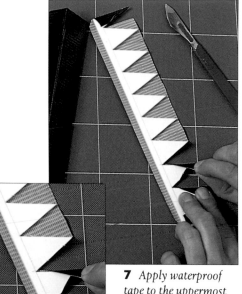

7 Apply waterproof tape to the uppermost surface of the card tunnel and to one side of the serrated strips. Trim the pointed edges neatly to keep them sharp.

8 Glue the tunnel and serrated strips to the centre of the casting frame as shown. Set aside.

9 Blend your pulp in an electric mixer, adding squares of soaked half-stuff in small batches.

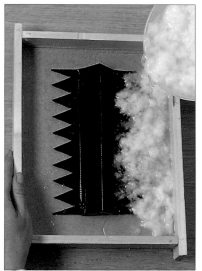

10 Strain the pulp over a plastic container to remove the excess water. Transfer the pulp to a bowl.

11 Pour the strained pulp slowly over the shape in the frame. It will not pour smoothly and will tend to splash.

12 Once the bottom of the box is covered, start to firm the pulp down with your hands, making sure you remove any air bubbles.

13 Sponge the surface of the pulp to soak up excess water. Keep the bowl into which you strained the pulp on hand, and squeeze out the sponge into it.

14 Build up the pulp over the higher areas of the shape by hand, pressing firmly to make sure the pulp adheres.

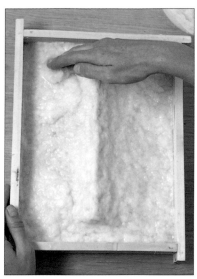

15 As a final check, feel for any thinner areas of pulp and add more if it seems necessary.

16 Sponge off any excess moisture, and allow to dry naturally in the frame. Drying time will depend on the thickness of the pulp and the surrounding temperature – it could take several days, or longer.

17 When the paper is dry, run a craft knife around the edge to break the silicone seal. Unscrew the frame.

18 Carefully slide a spatula under the corner of the paper in order to lift it from the base board.

139

Papier mâché

Papier mâché is a medium that is versatile, inexpensive and easily mastered. Its name is French for 'chewed-up paper' referring to the two methods of making papier mâché: from roughly torn paper strips or from a paper pulp. The first method is more common, because it uses basic household materials and needs no preparation. Papier mâché can be made into bowls, jewellery, wall ornaments, dolls, masks and headdresses. It can also be a convincing substitute for traditional sculpture. Shape an armature of chicken wire to your chosen form, and layer it with papier mâché. Or cast your sculpture from a clay model or existing mould, such as a fruit or shell.

A papier mâché object is made by building up layers of glued paper strips on a mould or by using papier mâché pulp. When the layers are dry, the form is eased from the mould and decorated. Newspaper is a good material for papier mâché, because it is flexible when wet with glue. The layering and the paste give it strength, and its tendency to discolour – normally a disadvantage – does not matter because it will be painted. The newspaper must be torn, not cut, because the slightly irregular edges blend with less obvious seams when the strips are pasted down. To make objects from papier mâché you will need to make a mould. The easiest way of doing this is first to make a model from modelling clay, then to cast a mould in plaster of Paris. You will find it useful to acquire a couple of simple modelling tools. These come in a variety of sizes with wooden or wire ends and are useful for shaping the clay and separating the model from the mould.

When the form is released from the mould it can be trimmed and bound with additional torn paper. After preparing the surface with paint primer or gesso – a mixture of chalk, white pigment and glue – you can then decorate your finished piece with poster colours or acrylic paint.

- ✓ Hand blender
- ✓ Paint brush
- ✓ Small scissors
- ✓ Craft knife
- ✓ Plastic buckets and bowls
- ✓ Rubber gloves
- ✓ Sieve
- ✓ Waterproof tape
- ✓ Modelling tools
- ✓ PVA glue
- ✓ Wallpaper paste
- ✓ Vaseline
- ✓ Modelling clay
- ✓ Gesso
- ✓ Acrylic paints
- ✓ Varnish
- ✓ Plaster of Paris
- ✓ A variety of newspapers and waste paper torn into strips

LAYERED DECORATION

These colourful pots and dishes were decorated with paint and cut-out paper shapes. The artist layered the cut-outs directly on to the pots and sealed them under a coat of varnish.

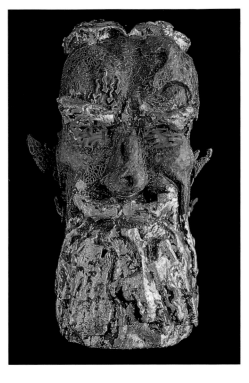

CLAY MODEL CAST

The direct cast technique of laminated paper with PVA glue over a clay model was used to create this extremely ornate mask. Tissue paper was used for the final layer to give a good texture for painting and varnishing (George Bernard Shaw Mask, Billy Nicholas).

WIRE FRAME CAST

This paper-only sculpture was constructed from paper pulp built onto a chicken wire frame, then painted and varnished (Louise Vergette).

ARMATURE CAST

The sense of fun and attention to detail in this artist's work is created by his observation of the human figure and all its gestures. The method of construction is similar to the previous piece but here he builds up an armature of cardboard boxes covered with newspapers to create a life-size character (The Hiker, Philip Cox).

Laminating

There are countless natural objects to cast from, such as shells, stones, bottles, bowls or wall plaques. We have chosen a scallop shell, but whatever the item, the principle for casting is the same.

1 *Rub a releasing agent, such as Vaseline, over the entire surface of the object. Do not leave any uncovered spots or the object may stick.*

2 *Tear some 2.5–3.8 cm (1–1½ in) wide strips of newspaper in the direction of the grain. You should have enough to cover the object. Then tear each strip into 3.8 cm (1½ in) lengths.*

3 *Mix some wallpaper paste in a bowl and immerse the paper strips so that each piece becomes thoroughly soaked.*

4 *Beginning at an edge, apply a strip of pasted paper and smooth it into place with your forefinger. Add a second piece, overlapping the first by one third. Continue until you have covered the surface. Allow the paper to dry.*

5 *Tear some newsprint of a different colour to form the following layer. Alternating colours helps you to keep track of the number of layers.*

6 *Apply the second layer in the same way as the first. Continue until you have eight layers, leaving the paper to dry between each application.*

7 *When the final layer is dry, trim the edges of the cast with scissors.*

8 *Prise the cast from the mould, easing it away from the edges until it comes free.*

Reinforcing Edges

The newly made cast has a raw edge of paper layers that need to be reinforced to ensure that they do not come apart. This is achieved by applying one or two layers of pasted squares.

1 Tear some short strips of newspaper, a different colour from your last layer. Paste them over the edge of the cast, from front to back, smoothing them with your finger.

2 Proceed all around the edge of the cast, overlapping each strip by one third. One or two layers is sufficient for an item of this size.

PREPARING FOR PAINTING

Papier mâché objects can be painted by brush, sponging, ragging or spraying, but all methods need a white opaque base to give the colours vibrance. This is best achieved with gesso, which dries quickly and covers well, so you won't need multiple coats of paint to conceal the newsprint.

1 Apply gesso to the cast using a wide brush. Two coats should cover the newsprint and create a solid ground for your colour.

2 Paint on acrylic colour with the same brush. For a bright, uniform effect, apply the colour with full intensity. If you want a more subtle wash, dilute the paint before applying. You can then remove colour with a rag to leave just a hint behind.

3 Add texture by dipping a wrinkled kitchen towel or cotton rag into paint and dabbing it onto the cast. The painted surface takes on the imprint of the wrinkles.

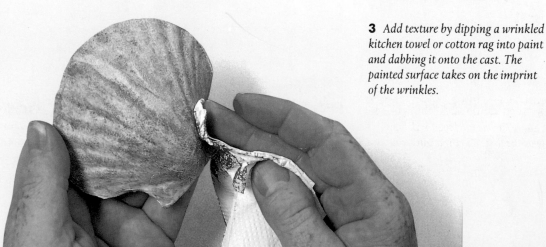

Making Papier Mâché Pulp

Pulping is an alternative to layered papier mâché that can be pressed into a mould or formed by hand. Its advantage is that you can build up thickness quickly instead of waiting for each layer to dry. You can also impress patterns into the pulp.

1 *Tear 2.5 cm (1 in) wide strips of newspaper with the grain, and tear again into 2.5–3.8 cm (1–1½ in) lengths. Half fill a plastic pail.*

2 *Pour about 1 litre (1¾ pints) of water onto the paper. As the paper absorbs the water, it will sink considerably.*

3 *Mix the paper and water with your hand or a plastic spoon to distribute it evenly in the pail.*

4 *Use a hand blender to pulp the paper. Stab the blender into the mixture in short bursts so not to clog. Proceed until you have reduced all of the paper fibres to slurry. Add water whenever the mixture seems too dry.*

5 *Pour the pulp through a sieve over a bowl to drain out the water.*

MAKING A SIMPLE MODELLING CLAY MOULD

To construct your own creations from papier mâché you first need to make a mould. One of the simplest and most convenient materials to use is modelling clay. Whether you are shaping a simple relief mould like the one demonstrated here or a complex three-dimensional mould where paper is layered on all sides – as shown in the Mexican project (pp.150–1) – you will find this an ideal medium to sculpt.

1 *Draw your design on medium-weight paper and cut it out to create a template. Place it on a slab of rolled-out modelling clay, and trace around the outside with a small wooden skewer.*

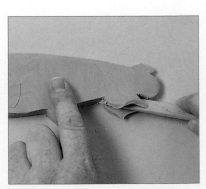

2 *Using a knife blade or wooden modelling tool, trim the excess clay from the scribed outline, then carve pieces away from areas that need thinning, such as the fish fins.*

Hand Pulping

Adding glue to pulp makes a modelling medium that sets hard and holds together well. You can use it on bowls, plaques and ornaments, or over chicken wire armatures to make sculptures.

1 *Pour about 285 ml (10 fl oz) of PVA glue into a bowl of pulp. (Wallpaper paste can be used instead.)*

2 *Disperse the glue evenly throughout the bowl of pulp with your hands or a plastic spoon.*

3 *Coat your mould with a releasing agent, such as Vaseline, and press the pulp onto it. Apply a small amount at a time, pushing it firmly into place with your finger until you have covered the surface with a uniform layer.*

4 *You can add pulp to form a rim, pinching it tightly together and pressing it into the main pulp.*

5 *Create a pattern with a wooden modelling tool or with your fingers. The finished piece can then be removed from the mould, gessoed and painted.*

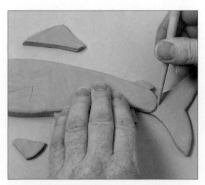

3 *Trace out details from your template and trim them to the desired thickness. Attach them by overlapping them slightly and smoothing the join with a wooden modelling tool.*

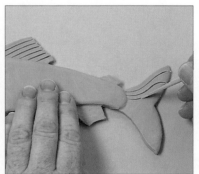

4 *When you are satisfied with the final shape of your mould, inscribe surface texture with various tools, or impress patterns using found objects.*

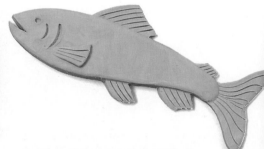

5 *Be careful not to create any sharp undercuts or over-projecting details that will prevent the release of the mould. Rub a releasing agent, such as Vaseline or liquid soap, all over the mould.*

Pre-Columbian Mask

ART FORMS

This project is cast by hand pulping from a plaster mould (see p.143). Because pulp is applied to the inside of the mould, all of the features show on the outside of the cast, in contrast to over-layering techniques that keep the detail within. A model is first made in modelling clay (see pp.144–5). It is preferable to choose a simple shape without projections that may hinder easy removal of the cast from the mould.

Pulp can take several days to dry in a plaster mould, and undergoes some shrinkage. But when it is dry, the cast can be primed, decorated with various materials and painted. A coat of varnish will seal it and allow cleaning with a damp cloth.

The plaque featured here is based on an image of Ehecatl, the Huastec god of the wind. The original is in the National Museum of Anthropology, Mexico City.

You could paint the mould terracotta, add gold varnish, and then rub it back for an antique finish. Or, as we have here, paint the mould with a rich gold for an authentic Pre-Columbian effect.

Building a clay model •

Making a plaster mould •

Casting with pulp •

1 Use a plastic board for making your model. Complex images can be built up from simple rolled shapes. Use a modelling tool to incise details. Avoid tight corners or undercuts that could hinder removal from the mould.

2 Cut some strips of waterproof material at least 1.3 cm (½ in) higher than the model, and build a wall around it.

3 Fix the walls in place with waterproof tape so that plaster will not leak through, taking special care to seal the corners.

4 You should rub Vaseline over the modelling clay. The Vaseline will act as a releasing agent.

5 Mix plaster of Paris to the manufacturers' instructions. A plastic bowl and spoon will be easiest to clean. Always wear gloves when working with plaster of Paris as it is an irritant to the skin.

6 As soon as the plaster is a smooth, creamy consistency, pour it over the clay model, filling to the top of the wall. Bang the work surface around the mould to bring air bubbles to the surface. Bubbles will form holes in the mould.

7 *When the plaster is dry, remove the wall, and set the mould aside to cure. When the mould is cold and hard it is safe to remove the clay.*

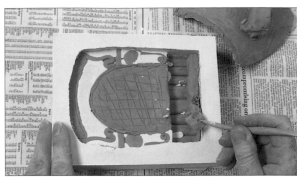

8 *Carefully extract the clay from the mould, using a wooden pottery tool. Try to remove large pieces to avoid damaging fine detail in the mould.*

9 *Dig out remaining fragments with the tip of the pottery tool.*

10 *When the mould interior is completely clean, apply a light coating of Vaseline to the entire surface.*

11 *Tear enough squares of white paper to half-fill a small bucket. To add colour, you can use watercolour paper. Add 1.4 litres (2½ pints) of water and blend.*

12 *When the pulp is a smooth creamy consistency, strain it to remove excess water.*

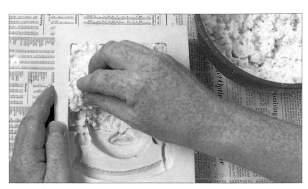

13 *Transfer the pulp to a clean bowl. Add some wallpaper paste and mix well.*

14 *Take a handful of pulp and push it into the mould with your fingers. Make sure you press pulp firmly into all the detailed recesses as you fill the mould.*

15 *Continue pressing pulp into the mould until it is full, squeezing out any air pockets as you do so.*

16 *When the pulp has dried completely, remove the cast from the mould. Depending on the size of the cast, the pulp may take up to two weeks to dry out.*

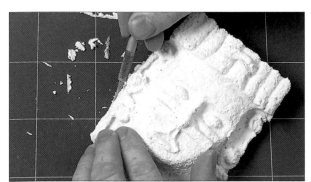

17 *The pulp will shrink significantly as it dries. Trim off any loose pieces to neaten the outline.*

18 *Apply gesso or acrylic paint to seal the mould.*

Mexican Folk Art

Modelling a standing sculpture in clay ●

Casting from a model by laminating ●

ART FORMS

This project is cast by laminating, or building up layers of paper (see p.140). This technique produces a stronger, lighter cast than the papier mâché pulp method on pages 144–7, making it a more suitable technique for a free-standing figure such as this.

To make a free-standing figure like the Mexican folk art parrot, you will first have to make a model out of modelling clay (see pp.144–5). The cast is formed by layering paper over the model, cutting the cast in two, removing the clay and rejoining the halves. This technique is popular because it is versatile, light and inexpensive.

Our project has been painted. However, you can obtain interesting effects by using colour comics, and then varnishing the finished cast to preserve the collage-like surface.

If you experiment with different types and strengths of paper you will find that layering offers a whole range of exciting possibilities.

Bright acrylic paints are in keeping with Mexican folk art and suit this project to perfection. This brilliantly coloured bird would look wonderful on a themed Christmas tree, or in a child's room.

1 *First shape the head and body. Next, form two wing shapes. Blend the clay together with a modelling tool. The bird was chosen for its simple shape; all you need is a basic form.*

2 *When you are happy with the form, add a few details such as the eyes and the strip over the head.*

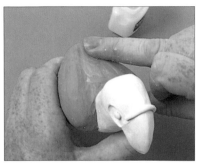

3 *Rub a coating of Vaseline over the entire surface of the mould to ease its removal from the paper cast.*

4 *Tear two different-colored newspapers into manageable pieces that will conform to the mould details without wrinkling, and mix a medium-size bowl of wallpaper paste.*

5 *Cover the mould in a layer of paper squares, overlapping each piece and smoothing it thoroughly with your finger, so that all of the detail stands out. Leave to dry.*

6 *Apply a second layer, using the other colour so that you can spot any missed or thin areas. Proceed in the same way until you have eight layers of paper.*

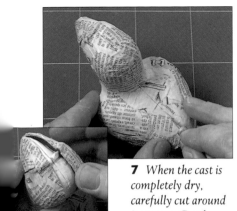

7 *When the cast is completely dry, carefully cut around its centre. Gently prise the halves apart and remove the mould.*

8 *Reunite the halves by pasting two contrastingly coloured layers of newspaper squares along the join.*

9 *When the parrot is dry, apply two coats of gesso to seal the cast.*

Paper Sculpture

Sculpture can be made from virtually any paper – recycled office paper, packaging or junk mail, or choose from the standard and special papers carried by art supply shops. As you will see from the works in this book, extraordinary sculptures can be created in myriad colours and textures. However, the epitome of this art form is still considered to be white sculpture, with its graceful modelling of light and shade. Such classic pieces are often constructed from top-quality hand-made watercolour papers whose high cotton rag content gives strength and malleability.

Unlike traditional sculpture materials, paper cannot be shaped into a compound curve, that is, a form that curves in two directions. When the second curve is made, the first curve springs back. However, you can create a similar effect by gluing two pieces of paper together. Most of the other restrictions inherent in paper can be overcome by careful cutting, curling, scoring and shaping.

Mastering the following techniques is crucial to success in this art form. Practise them thoroughly as a sound basis for your own creativity.

TOOLS AND MATERIALS

- ✓ Large scissors
- ✓ Small scissors
- ✓ Craft knife
- ✓ Cutting mat
- ✓ Pencils 2B and 6H
- ✓ Scoring tool
- ✓ Craft knife
- ✓ Wooden sculpting tools
- ✓ Eraser
- ✓ Stapler
- ✓ Small wooden skewers
- ✓ Tracing paper
- ✓ Wooden dowel
- ✓ Polystyrene
- ✓ PVA glue
- ✓ Silicone glue
- ✓ Various papers

SHADOW AND HIGHLIGHTS

*This delicate, all-white sculpture captures the elegance of paper sculpture in its purest form. Here the shapes are given life by the way each piece interacts with light and shade (*White Wreath, *Joanna Bandle).*

papers and then embellished some pieces further by adding painted colour to create a gradated tone, or a spattered background. These techniques further enhance a composition, giving an added illusion of depth in areas that may not be naturally modelled by light (Sally Jo Vitsky).

TEXTURED PAPER

A subject that is popular in any illustrative medium is the cat (above). Here simple, graphic shapes are given more interest by the use of fur-texture embossed paper (Rousseau's Cat, Clive Stevens).

THREE-DIMENSIONS

To create a three-dimensional effect the artist has cut and curled printing papers and then added texture with pastels. The frame becomes part of the composition (Wood duck, Bill Finewood).

153

...apes

...r sculpture shapes are created by cutting,
...folding and curling. Using combinations of
...sic shapes demonstrated here, you will be able
...nstruct more complex pieces.

...Scored lines are indicated on the diagrams by
...dotted lines. When scoring, it is best to bend paper
away from the scored line. When scoring alternating
valley and mountain folds (see p.53) you will need
to turn the paper over to score the correct side.

U SHAPE

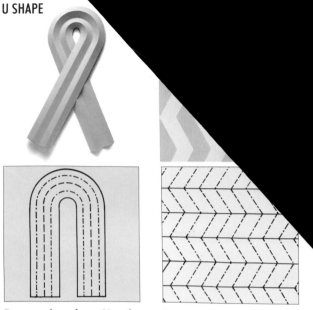

Cut out a large letter U and
score a valley fold in the
middle with a mountain fold
on either side. Pull one side of
the U over the other and glue
in position.

On a rectangular-shaped piece
of paper, score five vertical
marks, then score eight zigzag
horizontal lines with
alternating valley and
mountain folds.

SCORED CONE   CONE

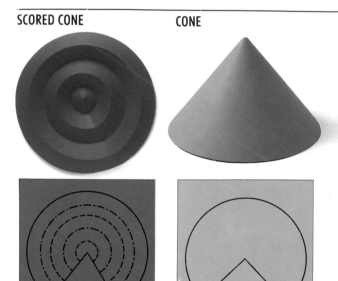

Cut out a circle and score
four circular lines, as shown,
to create alternating valley
and mountain folds. Cut out
a segment, pull the edges
together and glue.

Cut out a circle and remove a
quarter segment, then bring
the ends together to form a
cone and glue.

WAVY LINES

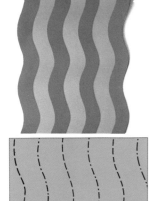

Cut out a rectangle with top and bottom edges as wavy lines. Score six horizontal wavy lines with alternating valley and mountain folds.

SWEEPING CURVE

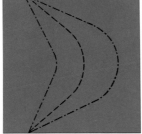

On a rectangular-shaped piece of paper score a curve from side to side to create a valley fold. Then score a corresponding curve on either side to create two mountain folds.

STAR

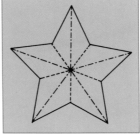

Cut out a five-pointed star. From the centre to each point, score a mountain fold. From the centre to the joint between each point score a valley fold.

FOUR FOLD

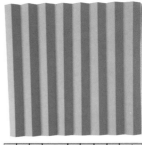

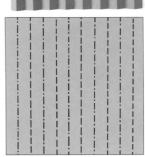

On a square piece of paper, score a series of equidistant horizontal lines for alternating valley and mountain folds. This is also called a fan fold.

TRIANGLE

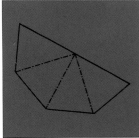

Draw four joining triangles, as shown, and score the dividing line between each. Fold along the scored lines and glue the fourth triangle behind the first.

CUBE

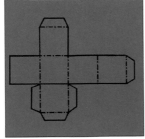

Draw the six squares, as shown, with glue tabs attached to them. Cut out and score all the joining lines and tabs. Fold together and glue tabs to attach.

CYLINDER

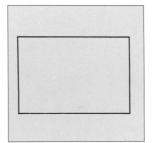

Take a rectangular piece of paper and curl over the edge of a table to form a tube. Open up and glue one edge. Bring the other end over to attach them together.

LEAF

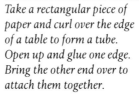

Cut out a leaf shape and score an S-shaped line along the central axis. Fold back to create a mountain fold.

155

Special lighting

Lighting plays a key role in modelling the elements of your sculpture, especially if it is all-white. This is important not only when planning and displaying your work, but when photographing it. Professionals use tungsten lamps, sometimes with coloured gels that bathe a white sculpture in tinted light. But you can achieve good results by photographing your sculpture in natural light. Choose a bright day but avoid brilliant sun, since this causes dark shadows. If one side is too dark, position a piece of white card near it, but out of camera range, to reflect light into the work.

However you light your work, it always looks best using only one light source. Experiment to find the situation and angle that suits each piece. The aim is to make the image appear to jump off the paper and to do justice to the originality of your work.

STRONG LIGHT – FLAT MOUNT

The lighting of the bee is not too far astray, but the piece lacks impact due to the mount being flat against the background.

FLAT LIGHT – RAISED MOUNT

Here the mount is raised but the light is too flat, creating an insipid look that fails to reflect the original.

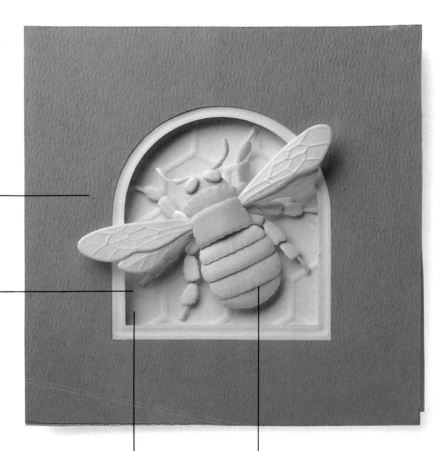

Good strong light gives an even overall colour.

Shadows under the wings are nicely diffused but give a convincing feeling of three-dimensionality.

Raising the mount off the background creates shadows that increase the 3-D quality.

The ribbed body is well defined with subtle shadows, as is the honeycomb background.

LIGHTING WHITE SCULPTURE

When photographing white sculpture, remember that since you do not have colour to define the form, your results rely purely on light and shade to model every detail. Therefore the positioning of the light source is vital.

SIDE LIGHT – FLAT MOUNT

The detail of the bee's body stands out under this lighting, but the effect is harsh and unpleasing.

SIDE LIGHT – RAISED MOUNT

This shot was constructed to show maximum modelling when lit. The result, however, is unbalanced; some parts of the modelling are sharp, while others are less distinct. The mount is flat and lacking in detail.

CREATING TEXTURE IN PAPER

PILLARS

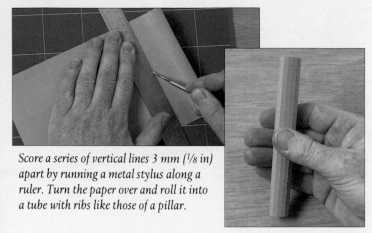

Score a series of vertical lines 3 mm (⅛ in) apart by running a metal stylus along a ruler. Turn the paper over and roll it into a tube with ribs like those of a pillar.

SWIRLS

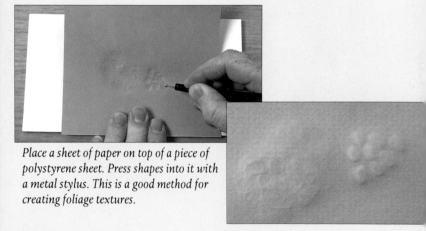

Place a sheet of paper on top of a piece of polystyrene sheet. Press shapes into it with a metal stylus. This is a good method for creating foliage textures.

STONES

Place some foam rubber in a flower press, and sprinkle small pebbles onto it as shown. Cover with a sheet of dampened paper and another piece of foam. Screw the press down securely, and leave for a day or two until the paper is dry. Remove the sheet. It will be textured with the imprint of the stones.

Adding Dimension

Raising components creates shadow and dimension, and results in a more interesting composition. Most relief paper sculptures use this method. Glue matchsticks, corrugated cardboard or a small block of polystyrene to the underside. This comes in 6 mm (1/4 in) and 3 mm (1/8 in) thicknesses. If you want a greater depth, sandwich several layers with glue.

USING MATCHSTICKS

1 *To raise small components, use a craft knife to cut matchsticks to length.*

2 *Glue the matchsticks to the back of the shape.*

BLOCKING SHAPES

3 *For larger components, apply polystyrene sheet in the same way to provide a strong and light support. Corrugated cardboard would also be a suitable material.*

4 *The resulting shape stands out from the surface, casting a natural shadow that gives the composition a wonderful sense of depth.*

Note the shadows cast by raising the figures.

GLUING POINTS

When assembling paper sculptures, it is important to consider all the elements of the construction, not just the parts visible in the finished piece.

1 *If you cut out this pencilled image exactly, you will not have sufficient overlap to glue the leaves together. You must therefore extend the leaf that sits underneath to make it the gluing point for the other leaves.*

2 *Place a dab of glue on the single leaf and attach it to the back of the double leaf. Press for a few seconds between your finger and thumb until the adhesive sets.*

Making an Armature

Three-dimensional objects often need an armature to support them. This can be made from cardboard, wooden dowels or chicken wire moulded to the shape of your sculpture (especially useful for papier mâché).

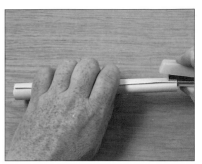

1 *Curl a rectangle of paper over the edge of a table. Press it with one hand while pulling the paper sheet down with the other hand.*

2 *Roll the curled paper into a tube, and staple the ends in place.*

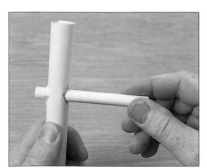

3 *Repeat to create a smaller tube, but this time glue it together—a stapler will not fit.*

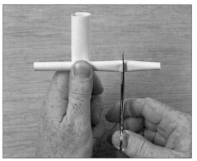

4 *Hold the small tube in position across the larger tube, and cut it to length with scissors.*

5 *With a sharp knife make an incision in the larger tube where the crosspiece is to be inserted. Do this in both sides of the tube. Make sure your fingers are safely out of the way.*

6 *Push the smaller tube into place through the incisions.*

7 *The tube opens the cuts just enough to pass through, and will therefore be held tightly.*

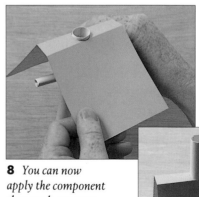

8 *You can now apply the component that needs support.*

Fashion Model

Creating a fully rounded sculpture •

Working with basic shapes •

Constructing the human figure •

ART FORMS

When building a free-standing sculpture, think of each component as a basic geometric form: a cube, a cylinder or a cone. Most shapes can be derived from these. A human body can be created from a cube with tapered sides, a head from a cylinder with facial features, and arms and legs from tapered cylinders. However, sculpture 'in the round' is considered difficult because you cannot rely on a single perspective sketch of your subject. You must consider the back and sides of each cut-out element, and where to add gluing tabs. Keep your shapes simple and within the limitations of the medium. Remember to allow for the spread of your sculpture, that is, the entire wrap-around area. The shape of a head mask, for example, that will look normal when curled around from ear to ear, appears unnaturally wide when flattened out.

Use paper that is sturdy enough to support the sculpture: the larger the sculpture, the heavier the paper. Keep your scoring neat – a messy line can mar the finished effect – and avoid halfway creases when curling and shaping. Gluing is easier if you clamp pieces with rubber bands and paper clips until set. With a little practice you will begin to construct complicated shapes.

The shades of mauve and purple enhance the sophisticated appearance of this paper sculpture. The colours of your sculpture should always be chosen with the final effect in mind.

TEMPLATES

Make an enlarged photocopy of the templates to the size you require and trace each one onto a sheet of medium-weight tracing paper with a 2B pencil. Remember that continuous lines indicate cut lines, and dotted lines show lines to be scored.

WORKING DRAWING

Start by sketching your sculpture. From this draw your templates, isolating manageable sections of the figure.

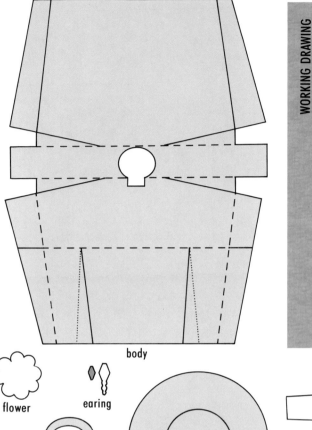

body

neck

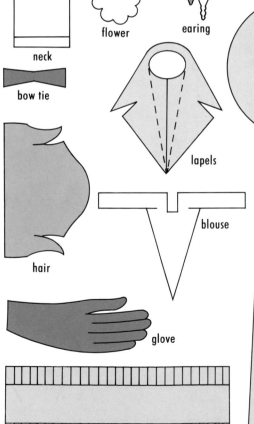

flower

earing

bow tie

lapels

hat

nose

face

lips

hair

blouse

glove

hat

sleeve

neck

1 *Cut out the main body piece. Cut through all the continuous lines with a sharp blade, and use a metal stylus to score the broken lines.*

2 *Fold all the tabs along the scored lines and then flatten the folds with your thumb.*

3 *To create a neat centre fold for the shoulder, place a ruler along each shoulder line and fold up against it.*

4 *Fold the body into its finished shape and check that everything fits snugly before gluing.*

5 *Glue the two pleats in the front of the chest and adhere to the gluing lines. Paste the shoulder tabs in position.*

6 *Glue the side tabs together, and attach as shown.*

7 *Complete the body by pasting and adhering the small tabs at the top of the arm position.*

8 *To make the neck, take a tapered rectangle of pale flesh-coloured paper and curl it over the edge of a table. Roll the sheet into a tapered tube and staple at the bottom only. This will allow the top to be adjusted if necessary.*

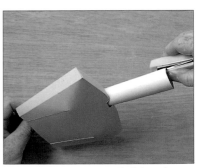

9 *Insert the narrow end of the tube through the neck hole and glue into position. Adjust the diameter of the tube to fill the opening and staple it.*

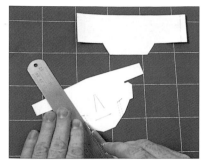

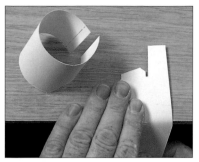

10 Cut out the two flesh-coloured head pieces, incising the slits for cheeks, mouth and nose. Score and shape the two lines on either cheek.

11 Curl both the head pieces over the table edge as before.

12 Using a thin wooden dowel, curl the ears forward slightly. Check their position from the front and adjust.

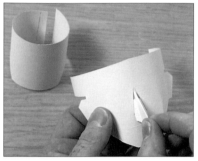

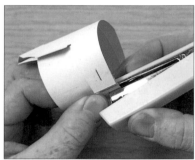

13 Cut out the nose and score down the centre to form a mountain fold with a valley fold on either side to serve as fixing tabs. Insert the nose into the head slots and glue from the back.

14 Glue the other head piece together. This will act as the foundation for the main head piece.

15 Staple the main head piece to its foundation by the tabs at either side of the head as shown.

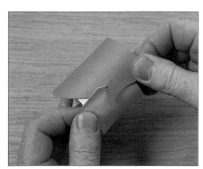

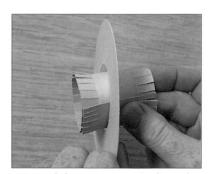

16 Cut out the hair and curl it around the back of the head. Connect the slits over the ears and staple into position.

17 Cut out the hat parts, and score and fold the hat strip. Make a series of cuts 3 mm (1/8 in) apart along the fold edge on either side of the strip.

18 Curl the strip into a cylinder and insert it through the brim. Adjust the diameter to fit, and glue into position.

19 *Fold back the glue tabs and attach them to the brim.*

20 *Fold down all of the tabs on the crown of the hat and glue the top disk over them. Turn the hat upside down and firm the tabs into position.*

21 *Cut out, curl and attach the hatband, gluing the joint at the back.*

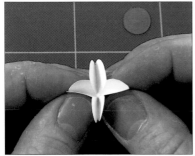

22 *Cut out and shape the flower, using four scored lines: two on one side and two on the reverse.*

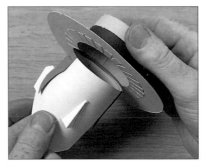

23 *Place the hat on the head. There is no need to glue it if it fits snugly.*

24 *Paste the back of the flower, and fix it to the hatband. Dot the middle with glue and add the purple centre.*

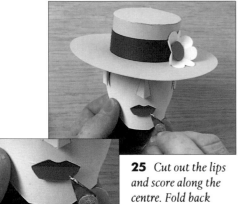

25 *Cut out the lips and score along the centre. Fold back slightly and glue to the mouth slit.*

26 *Glue the shirt front to the jacket. Curl the collar around the neck and glue at the back.*

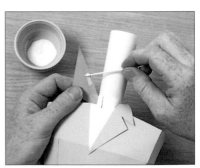

27 *Adhere one side of the lapels to the bottom of the shirt. Curl the lapel around the neck, then glue the end over the first point at the bottom.*

28 Cut out arm pieces, curl and glue into tapered cylinders. Round the top of the arms with scissors, put some glue inside and pinch together to attach.

29 Cut the left arm to length, glue at the top and fix to the side of the body.

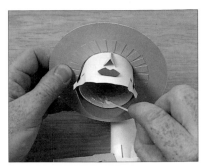

30 Glue inside the back of the head, and position it on the neck so that the chin protrudes.

31 Cut a V from the middle of the right arm to create an elbow joint. Cut out the mauve glove.

32 Glue the inside of the V cut in the upper arm, then bend the lower arm up and hold in position until the glue sets. Cut the hand over a dowel.

33 Glue the right arm to the body, holding it firmly so that it remains flat.

34 Glue the hand to the wrist, then carefully curl the fingers over and attach them to the hat brim.

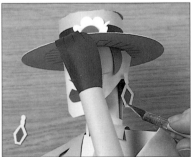

35 Assemble the earrings, glue at the back, and secure to the ears.

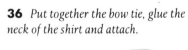

36 Put together the bow tie, glue the neck of the shirt and attach.

Bird in Flight

ART FORMS

Relief sculpture achieves its illusion of depth by using shapes cut out in perspective and elaborated at varying levels to create a natural shadow when the work is lit. This method has become popular in modern advertising and book illustration as an alternative to painting or drawing. Some contemporary paper sculptors will use only white paper to create the classic works that capture the essence of the medium and rely on light and shade to model their graceful lines. Others exploit the full range of coloured and textured papers, or use recycled materials, such as corrugated cardboard, newspapers, paper towels and cardboard tubes. Your choice is virtually unlimited. If flimsy paper would achieve a particular effect but is too light to shape, laminate it to a heavier material, such as watercolour paper — remnants of this are sometimes available in art supply shops.

Polystyrene sheet is one of the most convenient methods for elevating components, because it is light, easy to cut and glue, and holds its shape well. Mount your completed sculpture on a backing board and frame it to last for years.

Creating a relief sculpture •

Scoring and curling in sculpture •

Constructing a sculpture over a drawing •

The finished sculpture can be mounted on a backing board and then framed.

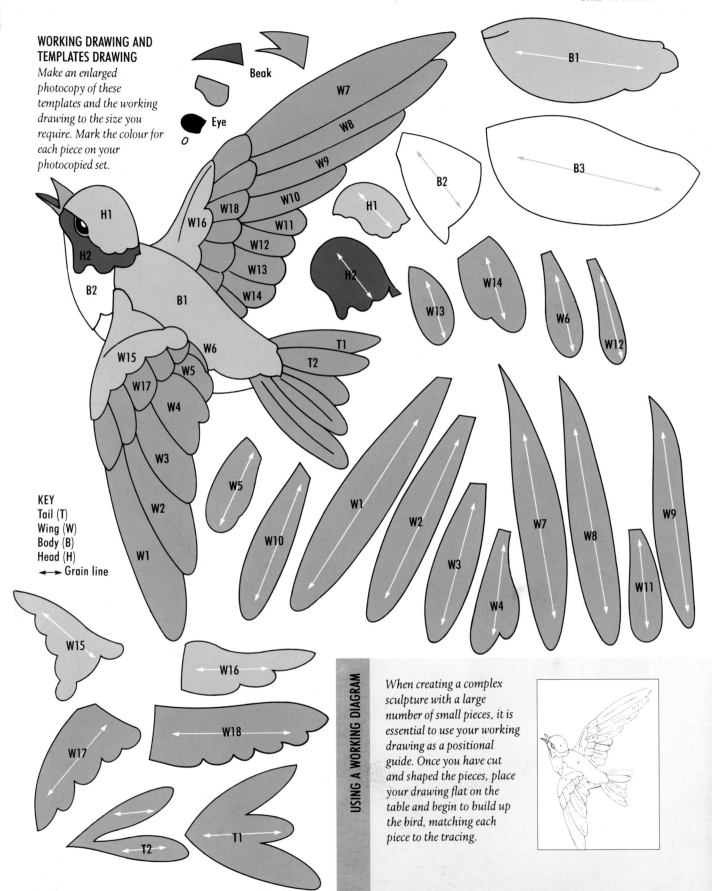

WORKING DRAWING AND TEMPLATES DRAWING

Make an enlarged photocopy of these templates and the working drawing to the size you require. Mark the colour for each piece on your photocopied set.

Beak

Eye

H1

H2

B2

B1

W18

W16

W15

W6

W17

W5

W4

W3

W2

W1

W7

W8

W9

W10

W11

W12

W13

W14

H1

H2

T1

T2

B1

B2

B3

W14

W13

W6

W12

W1

W2

W3

W4

W7

W8

W9

W11

W5

W10

KEY
Tail (T)
Wing (W)
Body (B)
Head (H)
← → Grain line

W15

W16

W18

W17

T1

T2

1 *Trace the diagram from an enlarged photocopy, and mark the colours.*

2 *Turn the tracing face down on a sheet of blue paper, and trace the outline of the wings with a hard pencil. Make sure you follow the grain of the paper and you leave enough overlap for the back wing to hide under the body (see template).*

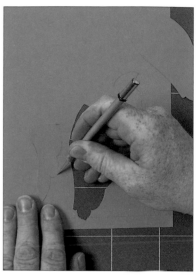

3 *Trace all of the blue parts. Cut them out and put them aside.*

4 *Cut the main body slit as indicated on the template. This is the connecting slit that fits around the bird's neck.*

5 *Curl the main blue body part over the edge of a table two or three times to ensure an even curve.*

6 *The smaller pieces are easier to curl around a dowel.*

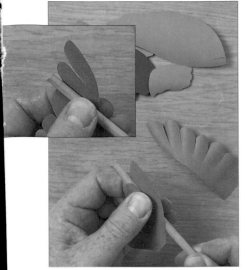

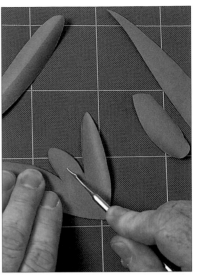

7 Cut and shape the red head piece, then the grey wing parts. Curl each feather in the wing piece over the dowel individually.

8 Cut the remaining grey pieces, and curl each one lengthwise.

9 Take the grey tailpiece and score a central line along each feather. Bend the lines back to form a mountain fold.

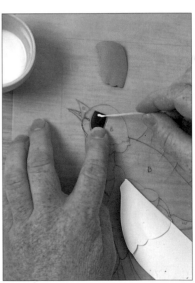

10 Repeat this scoring and folding process on the wing feathers.

11 Cut and shape the white breast and body pieces. Glue the top straight edge only and adhere to the white body. Note how the bird is built up using the tracing as a guide.

12 Cut and shape the black eye piece. Glue the top edge as shown, and attach the blue head piece to it.

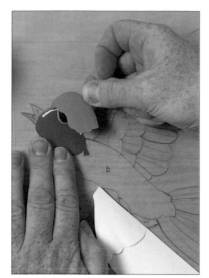

13 *Secure the blue cap with eye to the red head piece. Apply a strip of glue around the top edge only, so that the head does not sit too flat.*

14 *Assemble the beak parts and attach to the underside of the head as shown.*

15 *Taking the main body part in one hand, and the head in the other, slide the two pieces together, ensuring that the tabs interlock as shown.*

16 *Turn the assembly over and glue the back of the red tab. Hold in position for a few seconds to adhere.*

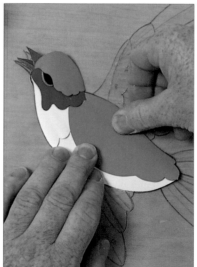

17 *Glue the top straight edge of the white body part and attach the blue body and head, smoothing the glued area with your thumb.*

18 *Cut out a tiny white oval, and glue it to the top of the eye to indicate the reflection of light.*

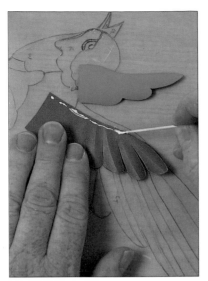

19 *Glue the top edge of the grey back wing feathers and secure the blue front feathers to it.*

20 *Glue the end of each grey primary feather in turn and attach to the underside of the wing assembly. Use your tracing as a position guide.*

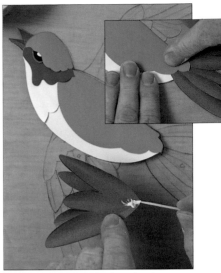

21 *Glue the two feathered tail parts on top of the three feathered pieces. Slide the assembled tail between the blue and white body parts, and glue the tail into place.*

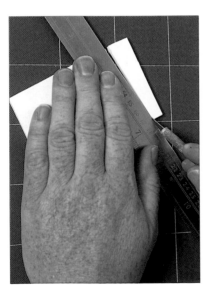

22 *Cut some tapered lengths of 6 mm (¼ in) polystyrene sheet to act as blocking for the wings.*

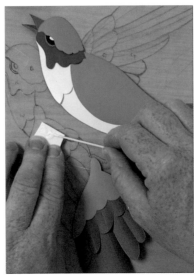

23 *Glue a 2.5 x 1.3 cm (1 x ½ in) block of polystyrene to the underside of the front wing. Then glue the other side of the block and attach it to the body.*

24 *Glue a similar block to the front of the back wing and attach the wing to the body.*

Storage and Display

ART FORMS

When you have completed your work you may want to display it. Flat pieces of art can be framed in the conventional way, but many pieces will be three-dimensional, and so present a greater challenge.

Works that are designed to be viewed from one side only can be displayed in a deep shadow box frame. You can buy these ready-made at a framing store, but the depth of the moulding is usually no more than 3.8 cm (1½ in), so you may have difficulty with bulkier pieces. You can have your work professionally framed to fit, or you can make your own, following the instructions given for the Menagerie Sampler on pages 48 to 49.

Larger pieces, or pieces designed to be viewed from all sides, such as sculptures, should be placed on flat surfaces. You may even want to use a turntable of some sort to facilitate easy viewing. Paper is a delicate medium, so if you are concerned about dust or moisture damaging your work, you may prefer to protect it in a glass display case. Remember that good lighting is paramount – for advice on how to light your work, see page 158.

Deciding whether to buy a clip-on frame or something more elaborate depends on your budget.

REPAIRING YOUR WORK

You can make minor repairs to your work if the paper becomes torn or if your papier mâché and paper sculpture creations get squashed or dented:

- *For tears, apply a thin layer of glue to a small strip of medium-weight card. Slide the card between the tear to transfer the glue and remove. Carefully press the torn pieces together or burnish down with a roller.*

- *To reinforce weak points caused by folds or thin areas from the papermaking process, paste a piece of thin paper, such as tissue or thin bond, to the back of the damaged paper.*
- *To repair dents, insert a dowel or knitting needle inside the piece and carefully push the dent outwards.*

You may not want to keep your art on permanent display. Even if you are less than happy with the results, do not discard any project. The versatile nature of Paper Craft lends itself to recycling, and so you may be able to incorporate your early attempts into future projects. At the very least, they will prove useful for reference.

A flat file is ideal for storing large pieces of flat work.

Flat pieces can be stored in a folder and put in a plan chest or flat file.

Any work that is not flat should be wrapped carefully and placed in a box.

Index

Credits

Quarto would like to thank all the artists who kindly allowed us to publish their work in this book, including the following who provided demonstrations: Edwin Corrie, Sophie Dawson, Jennifer James and Paul Jackson.

We would like to thank Specialist Crafts Ltd., Leicester for loaning a mold and deckle for photography, Robert Cunning for making the frame on pages 48-9, and Dorothy Frame for the index.

We would also like to acknowledge the following owners of featured work (key: a = above; b = below): John Frost Historical Newspaper Service 8a; Whatmans plc 8b; The Japanese Gallery, London 9a; ET Archive 10b.

All project photographs are the copyright of Quarto plc.